Also by E. L. Doctorow

Creationists

E. L. Doctorow

Creationists

Selected Essays, 1993–2006

RANDOM HOUSE

New York

Published in the United States by Random House, an imprint of The Random House Publishing Group, a division of Random House, Inc., New York.

RANDOM HOUSE and colophon are registered trademarks of Random House, Inc.

The publication history for each of the essays in this work is located on page 177.

"E. A. Poe" was originally published as "Our Edgar" in the Fall 2006 issue of the *The Virginia Quarterly Review.*

Grateful acknowledgment is made to the following for permission to reprint previously published material:

THE CONTINUUM INTERNATIONAL PUBLISHING GROUP: "Heinrich von Kleist" was originally published in *The Plays of Heinrich von Kleist* (Continuum International) and is reprinted by permission of The Continuum International Publishing Group.

THE LITTLE BOOKROOM: "Harpo" was originally published in *Harpo Speaks . . . About New York* (2001: The Little Bookroom). Reprinted by permission of The Little Bookroom.

THE NATION: "The Bomb" was originally published in *The Nation* (August 21, 1995) and is reprinted by permission of *The Nation.*

THE NEW YORK TIMES: "Harriet Beecher Stowe's Uncle Tom" is an expanded version of a book review of *Harriet Beecher Stowe: A Life* by Joan D. Hedrick, originally published in *The New York Times Book Review* (February 13, 1994), copyright © 1994 by The New York Times. Reprinted by permission.

ISBN 1-4000-6495-3

Printed in the United States of America on acid-free paper

www.atrandom.com

2 4 6 8 9 7 5 3 1

First Edition

Book design by Simon M. Sullivan

Contents

Contents

Introduction

THIS GATHERING OF ESSAYS is a modest celebration of the creative act. It acknowledges composition as the reigning enterprise of the human mind; it affirms that we know by what we create. I attend here mostly to compositions that take the form of stories. I write such compositions myself, and so am interested in those who write them.

A novel or a play has its origins in the peculiar excitements of the writer's mind. These are powerfully felt, even inspired, responses to what may be the faintest or most fleeting of stimuli—an image, the sound of a voice, a kind of light, a word or phrase, a bar of music. Or there may be an idea for which the writer has a strong sense of recognition, so strong that it becomes his to deal with as his domain.

Of course, not all—in fact very few—of the writer's states of arousal are resolved as finished works. Most are put aside for some mercurial reason: they are tried and found wanting in a page or so, or stashed away, or forgotten completely. But I imagine them as a kind of groundsong, these excitements, as constant and available as the sensation of life itself.

Wherever fiction begins, whether in the music of words or an impelling anger, in a historic event or the importunate hope of a justly rendered composition of one's own life, the work itself is hard and slow and the writer's illumination becomes a taskmaster, a ruling discipline, jealously guarding the mind from all other and necessarily errant private excitements until the book is done, the script is finished. You live enslaved in the piece's language, its diction, its universe of imagery, and there is no way out except through the last sentence.

Underlying everything—the evocative flashes, the dogged working of language—is the writer's belief in the story as a system of knowledge. This belief is akin to the scientist's faith in the scientific method as a way to truth.

Stories, whether written as novels or scripted as plays, are revelatory structures of facts. They connect the visible with the invisible, the present with the past. They propose life as something of moral consequence. They distribute the suffering so that it can be borne. To the skeptic who would not consider the story a reputable means of knowledge, the writer could point out that there was a time when there would have been nothing but stories, and no sharper distinction between what was fact and what was invented than between what was spoken and what was sung. Religion, science, simple urgent communication, and poetry were fused in the intense perception of a metaphor. Stories were the first repositories of human knowledge. They were as important to survival as a spear or a hoe. The storyteller practices the ancient way of knowing, the total discourse that antedates all the special vocabularies of modern intelligence.

There is a scientist in this book as well. Scientific formulas are revelatory structures of facts. They too connect the visible with the invisible. And, inevitably, they create realms of moral consequence. I argue here that the experience of discovering a scientific truth is for the scientist the same as the achievement of a realized work for the writer. In neither case is there a lingering sense of personal possession. The effort of one's mind seems, on completion, the work of outside forces. For all creationists, there is a strange displacement: the creative mind dissociates from what it has created. There is no memory of the effort involved. The book, the formula, becomes something *out there*, as if it appeared of its own volition.

I assume the experience is the same for the composer of music, the painter, the sculptor, the architect, the engineer. But the comedic mime, whose composition is in his physical deportment, whose revelations are composed as gestures, lives, like the dancer, in his expressive musculature, his art molded from his being.

Human creativity would seem to be rampant. From infancy the mind ascribes meaning to the unmeant; it lights what it sees and makes a home of the world. The results are not always benign. Our inventiveness is boundless and can be at its most dazzling as it breaches the moral imperatives we have created for ourselves. Like the communal composition out of Los Alamos, it can have horrifying consequences.

In the history of literature, some of the most beautiful, most profound works have been composed by the most wretched of souls; there is no necessary equivalence between the aesthetic and moral achievement of a novel and the confused, drunken, tormented, or immoral package of humanity who has produced it. Whatever sublimity inheres in the work does not necessarily exhibit itself in the author.

But the writers about whom I write do have a certain radiance in my eyes. I may not be uniformly positive in my judgments, but underlying all my attentions is a collegial homage, a sympathy, even a love for the aesthetic struggle as it shines with a kind of blessedness. After all, why compose fiction when you could be devoting your life to your appetites? Why wrestle with a book when you could be amassing a fortune? Why write when you could be shooting someone?

True storytellers ply their imaginations with a kind of self-questioning arrogance. They would reassert the authority of the single mind to render the world. They may not realize when they commit to the practice of fiction that they are ordained to contest the aggregate fictions of their societies. That, of course, is their redeeming value, but also an indication of the risk they take. It can be a dangerous profession, storytelling. If actuarial figures of writers' life spans worldwide were to be calculated, taking into account the jailings, the deportations, the executions, the disappearances, as well as the humdrum deaths from malnutrition and neglect, you would not want your son or daughter to become a writer.

Apart from such hazards, there is an entropic cost to the calling: writing is not merely a matter of setting down words. A novel is written at the expense of the novelist's being. Eventually, there is not much more to him that hasn't been written away. It may be the peculiar fate of the writer that after a lifetime of writing he becomes mysterious to himself, his identity having dissolved into his books.

Finally, the enterprise of writing gives no warrants. The few monumental works that change our thinking, our seeing, rise from the chatter of what is temporal, imitative, foolish, and easily forgettable. The writer will never know if his work will flash forth a light from his own time and place across borders and through the ages. His own time and place clutching and pulling at his feet of clay every day of his working life, he will know only how faint a light it is, and how easily doused.

And so, all in all, a degree of courage is involved in the practice even if the writer, as he flourishes in the realization of his first book, may not be aware of it. He will be taught about courage in any case. All creationists are mortal.

I.

Genesis

THE KING JAMES VERSION of the Bible, an early-seventeenth-century translation, seems, by its now venerable diction, to have added a degree of poetic luster to the ancient tales, genealogies, and covenantal events of the original. It is the version preachers quote from who believe in the divinity of the text. Certainly in the case of Genesis 1–4, in which the world is formed, and populated, and Adam and Eve are sent from the Garden, there could be no more appropriate language than the English of Shakespeare's time. The King James does not suffer at all from what is inconsistent or self-contradictory in the text any more than do the cryptic ancient Hebrew and erring Greek from which it is derived. Once you assume poetically divine authorship, only your understanding is imperfect.

But when you read of these same matters in the contemporary diction of the Revised Standard Version, the Jamesian voice of holy scripture is not quite what you hear. In plainspoken modern English, Genesis—especially as it moves on from the Flood and the Tower of Babel, and comes up in time through the lives of Abraham, Sarah, Isaac, Rebecca, and then to the more detailed adventures of Jacob and Rachel and Joseph and his brothers—seems manifestly of the oral tradition of preliterate storytelling out of which the biblical documents emerged, when history and moral instruction, genealogy, law, science, and momentous confrontations with God were not recorded on papyrus or clay tablets but held in the mind for transmittal by generations of narrators. And so Genesis in the Revised Standard Version is homier—something like a collection of stories about people trying to work things out.

The contemporary reader would do well to read the King James side by side with the Revised Standard. Some lovely stereophonic truths come of the fact that a devotion to God did not preclude the use of narrative strategies.

If not in all stories then certainly in all mystery stories, the writer works backward. The ending is known and the story is designed to arrive at the ending. If you know the people of the world speak many languages, that is the ending. The story of the Tower of Babel gets you there. The known ending of life is death: the story of Adam and Eve and the forbidden fruit of the Tree of the Knowledge of Good and Evil arrives at that ending. Why do we suffer, why must we die? Well, you see, there was this garden. . . . The story has turned the human condition into a sequential narrative of how it came to be; it has used conflict and suspense to create a moral framework for *being*. And in suggesting that things might have worked out another way for humanity if the fruit had not been eaten, it has, not incidentally, left itself open to revision by some subsequent fantasist who will read into it the idea of original sin.

Artistry is at work also in the blessings the dying Jacob bestows on his twelve eponymous sons. Each blessing, an astute judgment of character, will explain the fate of the twelve tribes led by the sons. A beginning is invented for each of the histori-

cal tribal endings known to the writer. Never mind that we understand from the documentary thesis of Bible sources—for it is,
after all, the work of various storytellers and their editors—that
different sons are accorded hands-on leadership by their father
according to which writer is telling the story. Character is fate.
And life under God is always an allegory.

Another venerable storytelling practice is the appropriation
of an already existing story. Otherwise known as adaptation, it is
the principle of literary communalism that allows us to use
other people's myths, legends, and histories in the way that
serves ourselves—Shakespeare's reliance on Hollinshed's *Chronicles,* for example, which should have, in honor, disposed him to
share his royalties. In Genesis, the ancient scribes have retooled
the story of the Flood recounted earlier in Mesopotamia and
Sumer, including the vivid rendition from the *Epic of Gilgamesh.*
Yet though the plot is the same, the resounding meanings are
different, as befits an adaptation. Noah is unprecedented as the
last godfearing, righteous man on earth . . . who may nevertheless drink a bit more wine than is good for him. And the God
of Genesis is a Presence beyond the conception of the Sumer-
ian epic.

The cosmology of Genesis is beautiful and for all we know
may even turn out to be as metaphorically prescient as some be-
lievers think it is. One imagines the ancient storytellers conven-
ing to consider what they had to work with: day and night, land
and sea, earth and sky, trees that bore fruit, plants that bore seed,
wild animals, domesticated animals, birds, fish, and everything
that crept. In their brilliant imaginations, inflamed by the fear
and love of God, it seemed more than possible that these elements and forms of life, this organization of the animate and

inanimate, would have been produced from a chaos of indeterminate dark matter by spiritual intent—here was the story to get to the ending—and that it was done by a process of discretion, the separation of day from night, air from water, earth from sky, one thing from another in a, presumably, six-day sequence culminating in the human race.

Every writer has to be in awe of the staying power of the Genesis stories, which have passed through the embellishing realms of oral transmission and the literate multilingual cultures of thousands of years. They are a group effort but not at all afflicted with the bureaucratic monotone that would be expected to characterize written collaborations. One reason for this may be the wisdom of the later scribes in leaving intact on the page those chronicles they felt obliged to improve upon. As a result we get more than one point of view, which has the effect, in the depiction of character, of a given roundness or ambiguity that we recognize as realistic. Consider Jacob, for example, who will wrestle with God or His representative and be named Israel, after all, but is impelled twice in his life to acts of gross deception—of his brother Esau, of his father, Isaac. Or the lovely, gentle Rebecca, who as a maid displays the innocent generosity that the servant of Abraham seeks, offering him the water from her water jar and then seeing to his camels . . . but who, years later, as the mother of Jacob, shrewishly assists her son in depriving Esau of his rightful patrimony.

In general, family life does not go all that smoothly for the founding generations. Beginning with Cain and Abel and persisting to the time of Joseph, biblical brothers seem—like the brothers in fairy tales—to be seriously lacking in the fraternal spirit. Wives who are not themselves sufficiently fertile foist slave women on their husbands for purposes of impregnation, and then become jealous of those women and have them sent away. There seem to be two stations of wife, high and low—Hagar and Leah being examples of the low—and the anger and resentment this creates is palpable. Overall the women of Genesis may be subject to an exclusively biological destiny as child bearers—theirs is a nomadic society that to survive must be fruitful—and the movable tent kingdoms in which they live may be unquestioningly paternalistic, but the modern reader cannot help but notice with relief how much grumbling they do.

It is in the pages of Genesis that the first two of the three major covenants between God and humanity are described. After the Flood, God assures Noah that He will not again lay waste to all creation in a flood. The sign of this covenant will be a rainbow in the clouds. Later, Abraham is commanded by God to resettle in Canaan, where he will be assured that he will eventually prevail as the father of many nations. Circumcision is the way Abraham and his descendants are to give sign of keeping this covenant. It is only in the next book, Exodus, that the final element of the covenantal religion—the Ten Commandments—will be given through Moses to his people. It is here that God will be identified as Yahweh and a ritualized sabbath—a simulation of God's day of rest after the Creation—is to be identified as the sign.

Apart from their religious profundity, this graduated series of exchanges between God and man has to remind us of the struggle for human distinction or identity in a precarious, brute life. This was the Bronze Age, after all. The Abrahamic generations were desert nomads, outlanders, who lived in tents while people such as the Egyptians lived in cities that were the heart of civilization. The ethnically diverse territory that Abraham and his descendants were called to was abuzz with Amorites and other Canaanite tribes. Under such difficult circumstances it is understandable that the Abrahamic nomads' desire to be a designated people living in a state of moral consequence would direct them to bond with one God rather than many gods, and to find their solace and their courage in His singularity, His totality. But that they did so was tantamount to genius—and a considerable advance in the moral career of the human race.

For finally, as to literary strategies, it is the invention of character that is most telling, and in the Genesis narratives it is God himself who is the most complex and riveting character. He seems at times to be as troubled and conflicted, as moved by the range of human feelings, as the human beings He has created. The personality of God cannot be an entirely unwitting set of traits in a theological text that declares that we are made in His image, after His likeness. There is an unmistakable implication of codependence. And this is no doubt some of the incentive for the idea expressed by the late Rabbi Abraham Joshua Heschel that the immanence of God, His existence in us, is manifest in the goodness of human works, the *mitzvoth* or good deeds that reflect His nature. "Reverence . . . ," says the Rabbi, "is the discovery of the world as an allusion to God." And so in reverence and ethical action do our troubled conflicted minds find holiness, or bring it into being. Recognizing the glory of God is presumably our redemption, and our redemption is, presumably, His.

2.

E. A. Poe

These are the tales of Edgar Allan Poe
Not exactly the boy next door

FROM *POETRY*
A ROCK OPERA BY LOU REED

EDGAR ALLAN POE, that strange genius of a hack writer, lived in such a narcissistic cocoon of torment as to be all but blind to the booming American nation around him, and so, perversely, became a mythic presence in the American literary consciousness.

His life was an unremitting disaster. Orphaned at the age of two, he was the dysfunctional adoptee of an unforgiving surrogate father. A gambler and a drinker, Poe was booted out of the University of Virginia. He took it upon himself to drop out of West Point. When he married it was to a cousin, a tubercular child of thirteen. Committing himself to the freelance's life, he lived at the edge of poverty. A Southerner, he stood forever outside the ruling literary establishment of New England.

Poe's baleful yet wary expression in his most famous photo shows a man who believed he was born to suffer. If circumstances in his life were not propitious to suffering, he made sure to change them until they were. Deep in his understanding, almost as to be unconscious, was a respect for the driving power of his misery—that it could take manifold forms in ways he didn't even have to be aware of, as if not he, but *it,* could create. That goes well beyond his conscious understanding of what he called the Imp of the Perverse—the force within us that causes us to do just what brings on our destruction.

His fiction can be so spectacularly horror-ridden as to suggest its origin in his dreams. Premature burials, revenge murders, and multiple-personality disorders abound. In proportion to his total output, Poe kills more women than Shakespeare. He kills them and they come back. They haunt, they avenge, they forgive. They are born one from another and merge again in death. Alive, they are entombed. Dead, they are dentally abused. Loved or hated, alive or ghostly, they are objects of intense devotion. Poe would claim, on occasion, to have written some of these pieces with enough distance to make him laugh. I don't believe that. In his "Philosophy of Composition" he says the supreme subject for a poem is the death of a beautiful woman. It can be, but it doesn't have to be. Another poet could write supremely of the death of a hired man. Another of the death of a civilization. In fact, as a poet, our Edgar is not the poet Melville is, to say nothing of Whitman or Dickinson. He is not major. He did not produce enough to be a major poet, and he may even be too much of a prim prosodist to be considered a minor poet. "The Raven" is to poetry as Ravel's *Boléro* is to music: rhythmic and hypnotic on first hearing, a mere novelty everafter. Or evermore. Nowhere in his ravenous mourning for Lenore does Poe come near the simple lines of one of Wordsworth's poems about the death of a young woman, "A Spirit Did My Slumber Seal":

No motion has she now, no force;
She neither hears nor sees;

Rolled round in earth's diurnal course
With rocks, and stones, and trees.

In these lines the poet does not claim an emotion; he gives us the means to create it in ourselves. Poe is usually a claimer. I have no great regard for his verse, though certainly his personality was that of "a poet to a T."

We do not move on from other writers of his century—Emerson, Hawthorne, Melville—as we move on from Poe. His love fantasies are, in their wild surmise, childlike. We read him young—for whom love is death and there is no one without the other—and go on from there. (I exempt Poe scholars who have found something the rest of us haven't. They argue for his work as Poe himself did. They take on his role of outsider. They suffer Henry James's opinion that "an enthusiasm for Poe is the mark of a decidedly primitive state of reflection.")

I do not forget that Poe wrote for a living. His output was prodigious—fiction, criticism, verse—and he was never unaware of what the market would entertain. (It was his lifelong dream to be the owner/publisher of a magazine.) Even in the steepest, most driven examples of his dark tales, he was fully cognizant of the gothic convention he was working. But if he wrote only for the money he would be like so many other hacks. If Poe is a hack he is a genius hack, genius being a kind of helplessness to do anything but flow through the brain circuits it has made for itself. Again and again he invents the imagery for impossible love, for unrelenting hate, for doom and despair. His contributions to the short story are the unmodulated voice—he starts high and ends high—and the embellished situation that serves for a plot. He pours the universal dread of existence into the forms of gothic fiction; that is what he does and it is the deepest source of his literary identity. It is why, when we think of Poe, we think of "Ligeia" or "Usher" or "William Wilson" or "The Cask of Amontillado" rather than his metaphysical treatise *Eureka* or the adventures of Arthur Gordon Pym. He is a test tube sample of the nature of creativity if any scientist wanted to boil it down to its salts: how we can be writing with both faculties of the brain, the surface, editorial intellect, and the impulsive, not clearly understood hallucinatory life produced in the brain's deepest recesses. So Poe knew what he was doing, and didn't know at the same time. He is an allegory for all literary life.

W. H. Auden, in his essay on Poe in *The Dyer's Hand,* believes Poe is ill served by the attention readers give to the gothic warhorses. He decides that the tales of destructive passion, such as "The Fall of the House of Usher," and the stories of ratiocination, such as "The Purloined Letter," are of a piece. "The heroes of both exist as unitary states—Roderick Usher reasons as little as Auguste Dupin feels." And neither has what Auden calls "an historical existence."

But there is an almost narcotized dream state imaging in the gothic pieces that even the fustian rhetoric cannot dim. Auden himself would seem to agree when he asserts that the "operatic prose" of Poe's horror tales is essential for preserving their illusion. All the more reason that readers would imprint on the supernatural stories of hideous passion and do no more than enjoy or admire the feats of ratiocination. We would still have Poe if he had never written a detective story. But we would not have him without his dead women and rotting manses and vengeful maniacs.

We mark the worst of his writerly sins in the stories that comprise his quintessential achievement. His overwrought style is so
filled with an essayist's rhetorical vines and brambles that you
have to slash and hack if you're to make your way through the
story. The verbosity, the undisciplined rhetoric, the drift into
haranguing essay, the purple passages—in sum, the grandiosity
of his tales—can sometimes seem intended only to assure Poe
of his own existence. I write, therefore I am. He likes to argue
his way into a story, finding presumably factual certifications—
usually three—for the tale he is about to tell. This recourse of
his not only delays the telling of the story the reader has every
right to expect from the very first line, it implicitly admits fiction's weak authority. I think of Poe's youth when, in the crises
of his gambling debts and academic failures, he attempted with
endless letters to persuade his adoptive father, John Allan, of his
merit. His rationalizations and bitter resentments pathetically
interspersed with his appeals for understanding (read money),
he strove for the lineal credentials denied him, and in the process
learned the art of self-justification. The tales may differ according to the identity of their narrators, or the time that passes
within each; there is always a crucial décor, and there is the loneliness of voice of the short story—the automatic circumscrip-
tion of the surrounding world that comes from the brevity of
the piece—and there is the drift to stasis in a story such as
"Usher," which is basically an elaborated situation. But a Poe
production is always unmistakably his. To find a rationale for all
his operatics in the so-called Europeanized bias of his writing is
to make a mistake: of a generation slightly in advance of Poe's
own, Heinrich von Kleist in Germany was writing tales that,
even in the heavily consonantal and syntactically burdensome

German language, raced along from one lean hunting-dog sentence to the next.

In contrast to Auden, another Poe critic, D. H. Lawrence, in his *Studies in Classic American Literature,* finds the gothic tales to be central to Poe's work, if only as evidence of his mental deterioration. Poe was "absolutely concerned with the disintegration processes of his own psyche . . . doomed to seethe . . . in a great continuous convulsion of disintegration and doomed to register the process," says Lawrence.

But Lawrence, being Lawrence, goes too far. On what grounds is Poe's psyche presumed to have deteriorated? He was the same Eddie from his first poems to the day he died. Does Lawrence deduce the deterioration from the work? But that would be to deny Poe the capacity of invention, the exercise of artistic choice, the strength of mind that is required to compose pieces from the mists of one's obsessions, what Poe in *Eureka* believed to be "the cool exercise of consciousness." Besides which, some of the strongest work came toward the end of Poe's life. The truly deteriorating psyche does not turn out hundreds of pages of fiction, verse, literary criticism, aesthetic theory, cosmogony. Poe's psyche, though in a state of permanent crisis, was stable. It was not my psyche and not yours, but it worked, it functioned. He made a life out of his profound orphanage. He was a strong enough personality to fabricate a family out of his teenage wife, Virginia, and Virginia's mother, whom he called Muddy, so that he had two women to love him in the entire range of a woman's love, as mother, as aunt, as girl-child, as sister, as cousin, as wife. Three hundred sixty degrees of attention. He could handle things, Edgar A. Poe. His every passing humor was their monumental concern. All together the three of them were a little constellation of misery. It ministered to his aggrieved soul. I know male poets today who arrange the world like that: they have their entourage, their devotees. They move like princes through their castles of suffering, with women strewing flowers before them and tendering hot water bottles at bedtime.

Lawrence's study of Poe does not bear close reading. He says Poe manifested only the "sloughing off of old consciousness" whereas another American writer of the time, James Fenimore Cooper, had the "two vibrations going on together, the disintegration of the old consciousness and the forming of a new consciousness underneath," because the "forming of a new consciousness underneath is the activity of American art."

But what exactly is Lawrence talking about? To speak of a deteriorating psyche is to speak clinically. To speak of a new consciousness is to speak philosophically, historically, geographically. A new consciousness is a social event, a revolution in perception. Perhaps Lawrence is thinking of the exotic foreign locales of Poe's fiction, the airless vaults, the heavy draperies, the crumbling houses. Whereas Cooper wrote of the French and Indian wars, the great outdoors of the North American woods. But why attribute to one setting the signs of a deteriorating psyche and to the other a new consciousness?

"Poe was going to get the ecstasy (of extreme spiritual love) cost what it might," says Lawrence. "He went on in a frenzy, as characteristic American women nowadays go on in a frenzy after the very same thing." Ah, those American women. "It is love that is the prime cause of tuberculosis," says D. H. Lawrence. Yes, he actually says that. Poor Poe, beleaguered by poverty, lack of recognition, and a dying young wife—as he wandered like an East Coast Ulysses from Richmond to Baltimore to New York to Philadelphia to Boston to Lowell, as he tottered back and forth, eternally disenfranchised, embattled, enraged, drunk, was he in danger besides of loving himself into a case of tuberculosis? Perhaps his wife, Virginia, was the greater lover, the characteristically more extreme and frenzied American female lover, because she did come down with tuberculosis. So Poe may have talked big, but she won the laurels.

Edgar Allan Poe was of the new American consciousness to a far greater extent than Cooper. He is as much an exemplar of the new consciousness, as much a formative master of the new world consciousness as Thoreau, Emerson, Whitman, Dickinson, or Mark Twain. As emotionally solipsistic as he was, and with little sympathy for the idea of a democratic republic, he was one of those American writers of the nineteenth century who were de facto prophets created by their new country to speak in its voice. They were not that far removed in time from the impertinent revolution and the still-breathtaking social reality of a land severed from kingship and so from the lineage claimed by kings. They understood freedom as unencumbered, though perhaps unblessed, by an ecclesiastical culture. Their personalities differed, and in literary address and in what interested them they couldn't have been more diverse. But each of their minds saw through to the metaphysical disquiet that comes with a secular democracy, a country written down on paper, a country in a covenant not with God but with itself. And whether in pain or gloom or elation or morbidity or bitter satire, they accepted it.

These authors could disdain the democratic mob around them, as did Poe, who, given all that room, all that sky and air, sent his words out from the sealed crypt of his own brain; or they could open their arms as rhapsodists, theologically self-

infatuated from the use of words, which was the case with
Emerson; or they could be self-consecrating, as Walt Whitman
certainly was, all his life the singer of himself. Twain, unlike
Hawthorne, did not find the tragedy in churchly rectitude; he
was a merciless skeptic for whom the ordinary pieties were a
form of fraud. Dickinson uses her words as stitches, as if life is a
garment that needs mending. And in Herman Melville—well,
there the reportage most dramatically anticipates much of the
twentieth century's. The universe he reports is as amoral and
monstrous as the featureless megalithic head of the white whale.

All of these voices together, were they one, would suggest a
bipolar mental disorder. Nevertheless, they comprise the demanding literary project of a secular nation. Poe's work no less
than the others' teases out the risky ontological premises of the
Enlightenment. Whatever his or any of his fellow authors' religious hopes or conflicts might have been, as writers they proph-
esy the modernist future implicit, if not entirely intentional, in
the documentations of the Founding Fathers.

The philosopher Richard Rorty has suggested that the meta-
physic of the American civil religion is pragmatism. To tempo-
rize human affairs, to look not upward for some applied celestial
accreditation but to look forward, at ground level, in the endless
journey, to resist any authoritarian restriction on thought—that
is the essence of the civil religion, an expansive human inquiry
that sees humankind putting all the work and responsibility for
the value of life on its own shoulders. Well, what is that idea,
what metaphor for it is more apt, than a son without a father or
a mother, the orphan being forever without consolation for his
existence, and the only love requisite to his longing beyond his
reach? On his own Poe essayed a poetics, a psychology, a cos-

mology that, all together, might be viewed as a grandiose at-tempt to fill in post-Enlightenment meaninglessness. It was irre-pressible, wild, excessive, and petrified. His poetics, which anticipated the New Criticism by a century, makes of poetry a humanly made artifice of sounds and rhythms and images. The derived and grandiose boyish cosmology of *Eureka* is his bible. And living in the freedom of the happiest and most advanced social constructions, in the democracy that Lincoln would call the last best hope of mankind, Edgar Poe with his dark tales laid out its unavoidable nightmares.

These are the tales of Edgar Allan Poe
Not exactly the boy next door

3.

Harriet Beecher Stowe's Uncle Tom

HARRIET BEECHER WAS BORN in 1811, the seventh child of the fervent Congregationalist preacher Lyman Beecher and Roxana Foote, a granddaughter of one of Washington's generals, a woman who read French and the scientific articles in the *Edinburgh Review*, but who died anyway at forty-one, the exhausted mother of nine.

The little girl grew up in the Connecticut towns of Litchfield and Nutplains with surrogate mothers from the extended Beecher and Foote families, most important an aunt, Harriet Foote, who taught her the beauties and strengths of a fading preindustrial culture and who gave her an empowering faith in the female mind that would serve her through all her coming adult struggles and competitions with the male. This endowment was enriched by her maternal uncle, Samuel Foote, a world traveler of great sophistication, who introduced such non-Congregationalists as Lord Byron and Sir Walter Scott to the Beecher children's library; and by her older sister, Catharine Beecher, who founded the Hartford Female Seminary devoted to the higher education of women at about the time Harriet, whom her father called the family "genius," was growing past the best her primary school had to offer. Catharine Beecher, who would make women's education her life's mission, brought her sister to her new school when Harriet was age thirteen.

The Hartford Seminary insisted on all the traditional subjects of the male curriculum—languages, natural and mechanical science, composition, ethics, logic, mathematics—but forswore the giving of awards or other male means of motivating students by competition. Instead, Catharine installed a system of sisterhood that called upon advanced pupils to teach the less advanced on the principle that whoever knew something should feel privileged to share that knowledge. In doing so, says her biographer Joan D. Hedrick (*Harriet Beecher Stowe: A Life*), she modeled the school on the Beecher children's custom of helping with one another's education. At home, their older brother Edward had taught Catharine Latin, Catharine had taught Harriet, and Harriet had taught her younger brother Henry. Now, in full acquiescence, the tiny teenage Harriet set about teaching her fellow students as well.

In 1832, Lyman Beecher, who had remarried and sired four more children, moved his enormous brood to Cincinnati, a Western boomtown that was on its way to becoming the sixth largest city in America. Lyman believed the West was where the battle for America's soul would be fought, a battle, he said, "in which Catholics and infidels have got the start of us."

Young Henry Ward Beecher, whose later fame as minister at Brooklyn's Plymouth Church would far outstrip his father's, compared this move to Jacob and his family going down to Egypt. None of the talented Beecher siblings, most of whom would come to live public lives always in the thick of things, could ever be accused of diffidence. But Harriet, with a satirical spirit developed at Hartford, where she had written mock heroic student newspaper editorials, detested the self-aggrandizing biblical allusions of the Beecher males, and wrote in a letter about the arduous journey by boat and stage: "Here we all are—Noah, and his wife, and his sons, and his daughters, with the cattle and creeping things, all dropped down in the front parlor of this tavern, about thirty miles from Philadelphia."

Harriet had always written well, with wit and fluency, but with no thought of herself as a writer. Now, to inform the friends and family relations back east of life in Cincinnati, she became an artful correspondent and more or less inadvertent chronicler of the new "national culture," says Hedrick, that was replacing the "regional culture" the Beechers had recently left behind. Her letters were filled with particulars of everyday life, descriptions of people, parlors, scenes on the streets. Almost effortlessly they formed a kind of epistolary novel, drifting from personal communication into literary discourse.

A second crucial factor in Harriet Beecher's development as a writer was the literary club. Having written a children's geography book with her sister Catharine, published in 1833, she was invited to join the Semi-Colons, a gathering of men and women who met every Monday evening for parlor readings by the members, discussion, dancing, and refreshments. For these occasions Harriet wrote sketches and stories that she read aloud, and for which she was praised, given advice, and criticized, much in the manner of a young writer today in a university writing workshop. This was a notch up from letter writing and the experience was invaluable.

"Parlor literature afforded Harriet Beecher an advantage she never lost," says Hedrick, "an intimate relationship to her audience. Her stories were always read aloud—in later years to her husband and children and servants—and as she gauged their effect she developed a powerful capacity to move her audience."

The Semi-Colon Club brought Harriet Beecher together with Calvin Ellis Stowe, an impoverished but highly respected biblical scholar and linguist, a widower whose late wife, Eliza, a victim of one of Cincinnati's periodic cholera epidemics, had been Harriet's friend. Harriet married Calvin in January 1836 and gave great merriment to the Beecher men by delivering twins the following September, an act they thought typical of her "eccentricity."

But as she knew from her own mother's experience, motherhood was far from a laughing matter. She was to have another child, a boy, within a year, and thus find herself with three children under the age of eighteen months, all of whom had to be nursed, guarded against illness, and maintained on the salary of an impecunious scholar. She began to write sketches for various magazines to supplement the family income, and from her earnings hired household help, black and white, to give herself the time to devote to more writing, a stratagem that anticipated the complex lives of working women today.

Calvin Stowe believed in a companionate marriage of equals, but knew himself to be demanding, emotionally explosive, and generally critical of his wife's household management. The Stowes more or less complicitly practiced birth control by abstinence, each of them taking trips alone for months at a time—Calvin to Germany to purchase scholarly libraries, Harriet to Connecticut, or Vermont, where she underwent the faddish water cure as much for relief from her conjugal and maternal duties as for the benefits of the regimen.

Despite their long periods of separation, Harriet would over the years bear Calvin seven children, one, Samuel Charles, breaking her heart by dying in infancy, and others bringing unassuageable grief to her middle and old age through their drunkenness, morphine addiction, or accidental death.

The Stowes' lifelong marriage would be loving if difficult, but the difficulty would be compounded by Harriet's celebrity as the author of *Uncle Tom's Cabin*. The immediate historical outrage that fired her up for the great work of her life was the Fugitive Slave Law, passed by Congress in 1850, which effectively suspended the rights of habeas corpus and trial by jury, made white America into a kind of standing posse, and punished with prison sentences and fines anyone who gave shelter or assistance to an escaped slave. In every city in the North, black people, free or escaped, were kidnapped in the street, or seized in their homes, and, without regard for due process, remanded to slavery.

Harriet had become embroiled in the abolitionist cause fifteen years before, when her father's seminary students publicly condemned slavery and when a pro-slavery mob in Cincinnati attacked and destroyed the presses of a local abolitionist paper; then she had written a letter to the editor of *The Cincinnati Journal*, using a male pseudonym, that defended abolitionism on First Amendment grounds. Now, however, the moral imperative she felt was all consuming. She conceived of a series of related sketches that would give a picture of slavery, and contracted to publish them in *The National Era*, a magazine for which she had written before. "The time is come when even a woman or a child who can speak a word for freedom and humanity is bound to speak," she wrote to the publisher.

Harriet thought the story she had to tell would last three or four numbers. In fact its installments ran weekly from June 1851 to April 1852. Published as a book in March 1852, just before the last installment was serialized, *Uncle Tom's Cabin* sold 10,000 copies within a week and 300,000 by the end of a year. In England, where there was no slavery, it was even more successful. Eventually it would be translated into more than forty languages, and became the second most popular book in the world after the Bible. It was also rendered into every imaginable form of kitsch the nineteenth century could contrive—stage melodrama, "song, theater, statuary, toys, games, handkerchiefs, wallpapers, plates, spoons, candlesticks."

One of the most impressive features of Hedrick's biography is her cogent analysis of *Uncle Tom's Cabin*. The source of its narrative voice, its domestic frame of reference, its use of dialect, and the "impulse to instruct" she finds in Stowe's earlier products of parlor literature, the only practicable kind given to one of a generation of women taught to keep their self-expression within the confines of the home. Its Christocentric life view was almost inevitable for a daughter and sister and wife of clergymen, and a righteous believer shocked by the sanctimonious rationalizations of pro-slavery Christians.

Hedrick makes no wild claims for *Uncle Tom's Cabin* on literary grounds. She concurs with the critics who have pointed out Stowe's unacknowledged appropriation of published slave narratives—particularly those by Josiah Henson and Henry Bibby—and she emphasizes the paternalistic racism of Stowe's stereotyping. But she argues for the story of Eliza's escape to freedom as countervailing to Uncle Tom's passive submission to his fate—pointing out that the book incorporates a "freedom narrative" as well as a slave narrative—and in a larger context she makes a literary historian's argument for all the book's internal flaws and moral self-contradictions as a mirror of the conflicted American nation.

But it is not the mirror of a conflicted nation one finds in reading the book now, some hundred and fifty years after its publication. There is something about it that goes well beyond, or beneath, the grim social realities of antebellum life. *Uncle Tom's Cabin* is a difficult book to stay with; it is too much of what it is, and the effect can be at moments a gloss on a Poe gothic with its love of what Poe calls "the single effect." Moralistic, tendentious, and unrelenting, it is a cause in book form with nothing in it that is not editorialized. It becomes at times iconic, more a crude woodblock print or stained-glass window than a novel. We feel the immensity, the tragedy of the subject, deserves something more.

For all her inventiveness Stowe flounders in the stasis of her unremitting idea—not just that slavery is evil, but that it defames God's shining Christian kingdom. The book's theologic temper relates it not as much to any of the prescient political novels of later times—Upton Sinclair's *The Jungle,* George Orwell's *1984*—as to the currently popular potboilers of evangelical fantasy. Either/or, says Stowe, either Heaven or the vengeance of the Lord; as much is said in the last chapter, entitled "Concluding Remarks," in which she attests to the truth of her revelations and calls in supporting witnesses, including her husband, "Professor C. E. Stowe," for certification. It is the "Church of Christ" that must heed her prophecy, lest Hell be the fate of the nation.

There are two intertwining plots—we can acknowledge that

the book enjoys that much of traditional fictive practice—one following Tom downriver to his eventual death at the hands of Simon Legree, the other following Eliza north across the Ohio River and with her husband, George Harris, to freedom. And we can also grant Stowe her gift for dialogue—she is never more free and relaxed than when giving in to her loving representations of malapropist black talk, or righteously hypocritical white talk, or when indulging the angelic reflections of Little Eva, the white child whom Tom saves from drowning but who will die subsequently, her impending death having no effect whatsoever on her sweet wise-child equanimity. And Tom has his biblical discourses as well.

With her address to the reader and her chapter headings, Stowe has clearly read her Dickens and her Fielding, though I don't believe they bolstered their chapter heads with biblical epigraphs. There is a self-indicative display of the writer's gifts in her habit of explaining the meaning of scenes she has just presented. That she could be transported by the act of writing is evident in a letter Hedrick quotes that Stowe wrote to George Eliot: "Did you ever think of the rhythmical power of prose, how every writer when they get warm falls into a certain swing and rhythm peculiar to themselves, the words all having their place and sentences their cadences?" Yet there was a moral demand, an urgency in her soul to speak out, and courageous as it was, it carries that visionary insistence that does not trust the intrinsic value of the fictive enterprise, does not trust it to do what the tract is sure to accomplish. Her book conceives for its major effects the presentation of "flat characters"—in E. M. Forster's formulation, characters who "in their purest form . . . are constructed around a single idea or quality." They are "easily recognized whenever they come in—recognized by the reader's emotional eyes, not by the visual eye which merely notes the recurrence of a proper name." While some of the greatest characters in literature are flat—Falstaff comes to mind—a preponderance of them in one novel gives it its editorial nature. Tom will always be forbearing, pious, and subservient. Little Eva will in every circumstance be angelic. And Legree is the one with the whip in hand.

It is wrong to think of Uncle Tom as "an Uncle Tom," though. In context, in the scheme of the book, he is the Christ come down again to live and suffer among the lowly. About to die, he says, "the Lord's bought me." Stowe has chosen the precise metaphor for the slavish son of God.

Withal, the implicit racism of Stowe's stereotypes in *Uncle Tom's Cabin* is more a cause for despair to me, I think, than to her biographer. It is an indication of how tortuous is the moral progress of a culture where even the religiously driven protest, the aesthetically organized act of moral intellect, assumes the biases of the system it would overthrow. Stowe's work reflects just what she opposed, its hideous customs and attitudes reflected in the very act of condemnation. The wide popularity and instant enormous influence of her book, which reports as news that black people are human beings, suggests a nineteenth-century society that could not work out that realization for itself, at least to the point of any practical effect on its behavior.

Hedrick makes much of the resistance to Stowe on the part of the Boston Brahmin and New York schools of male writers—everyone from Hawthorne to Henry James—who were concertedly striking popular women writers from serious literary consideration for not writing a purely aesthetic and distanced prose unencumbered by the impulse to instruct. It is illuminating, not to say instructive, to see how hard our nineteenth-century greats worked to put themselves and only themselves into the American literary canon. Whatever the merits or weaknesses of Stowe's fiction, she was, along with other women writers of the day, the victim of a quite deliberate and successful movement to divide American culture into the high and the low.

Yet for a good part of the nineteenth century *Uncle Tom's Cabin* swept high culture out the door. Abraham Lincoln met Harriet Beecher Stowe in 1862 and said, "So you're the little woman who wrote the book that started this great war!" Little she was, under five feet tall, but a parlor powerhouse of evangelical intellect who managed to draw through her life all the great moral and cultural struggles of her century. We are not wrong to apprehend the possibility of another moment to come when things are so corrupt, so monumentally inhuman in the life we've constructed for ourselves that only the low literary culture of Stowe's legacy will do—the overwritten melodrama, the gothic horror tract, as necessarily moralistic and as tendentiously engaged for its purposes as *Uncle Tom's Cabin* was for hers.

4.

Composing *Moby-Dick*
What Might Have Happened

I CAN CLAIM a personal relationship to Melville and his works, having read *Moby-Dick* three and a half times. The half time came at the age of ten, when I found a copy in my grandfather's library—it was one of a set of great sea novels all bound in green cloth—and it was fair sailing until the cetology stove me in. I first read the book in its entirety (and *Typee, Omoo, Billy Budd,* and "the Encantadas" and "Benito Cereno" and "Bartleby the Scrivener," for that matter) as an undergraduate at Kenyon College. Then, as a young editor at New American Library, a mass-market paperback publisher, I persuaded a Kenyon professor, Denham Sutcliffe, to write an afterword to the Signet Classic edition of *Moby-Dick,* and so read the book again by way of editorial preparation. And now on the hundred and fiftieth anniversary of its publication (and after too many years) I have read it for the third time.

The surprise to me, at my age now, is how familiar the voice of that book is, and not merely the voice, but the technical effrontery, and not merely the technical effrontery, but the character and rhythm of the sentences . . . and so with some surprise, I've realized how much of my own work, at its own level, hears Melville, responds to his perverse romanticism, endorses his double-dipping into the accounts of realism and alle-gory, and I'm in awe of the large risk he takes speaking so frankly of the crisis of human consciousness, that great embar-rassment to us all that makes a tiresome prophet of anyone who would speak of it.

Hawthorne I have always understood as a writer who affected me deeply, and I have realized my sometime inclination to write romances in the Hawthornian sense—novels set in the past that would cure up real life into a gamier essence. But whatever rule breaking I have done in my work I probably owe to Melville, Hawthorne's devoted admirer, but also his saboteur, in taking the elements of the well-constructed novel and making a cubist composition of them.

Literary history finds a few great novelists who achieved their greatness from an impatience with the conventions of narrative. Virginia Woolf composed *Mrs. Dalloway* from the determina-tion to write a novel without a plot or indeed a subject. And then Joyce, of course: like Picasso, who was an expert draftsman before he blew his art out of the water, James Joyce proved him-self in the art of narrative writing before he committed his as-saults upon it.

The author of the sterling narratives *Typee* and *Omoo* precedes Joyce with his own blatant subversion of the narrative compact he calls *Moby-Dick*. Yet I suspect that, in this case, the subversion may have been if not inadvertent, then only worked out tacti-cally given the problem of its conception. I would guess that what Melville does in *Moby-Dick* is not from a grand precon-ceived aesthetic (Joyce: I will pun my way into the brain's dreamwork; I will respect the protocols of grammar and syntax but otherwise blast the English language all to hell) but from the necessity of dealing with the problem inherent in constructing an entire nineteenth-century novel around a single life-and-death encounter with a whale. The encounter clearly having to come as the climax of his book, Melville's writing problem was how to pass the time until then—until he got the *Pequod* to the southern whale fisheries and brought the white whale from the depths, Ahab crying "There she blows—there she blows! A hump like a snow-hill! It is Moby-Dick!" She blows, I note, not until page 537 of a 566-page book, in my old paperback Rinehart edition.

A writer lacking Melville's genius might conceive of a shorter novel, its entry point being possibly closer in time to the deadly encounter. And with maybe a flashback or two thrown in. A novelist of today, certainly, would eschew exposition as far as possible, let the reader work out for herself what is going on, which is a contemporary way of maintaining narrative tension. Melville's entry point, I remind myself, is not at sea aboard the *Pequod,* not even in Nantucket: he locates Ishmael in Manhattan, and staying in scene every step of the way, takes him to New Bedford, has him meet Queequeg at the Spouter Inn, listen to a sermon, contrives to get them both to Nantucket, meet the owners of the *Pequod,* endure the ancient hoary device of a mysterious prophecy . . . and it isn't until chapter 20, which begins "A day or two passed," that he elides time. Until that point, some ninety-four pages into the book, the writing has all been a succession of unbroken real-time incidents. Another ten pages elapse before the *Pequod,* in Chapter 22, "thrusts her vindictive bows into the cold malicious waves."

I wouldn't wonder if Melville at this point, the *Pequod* finally underway, stopped to read what he had written to see what his book was bidding him to do.

This is sheer guesswork, of course. I don't know what Melville himself may have said about the writing of *Moby-Dick* beyond characterizing it as a "wicked book." Besides, whatever any author says of his novel is of course another form of the fiction he practices and is never, never to be taken on faith.

Perhaps Melville had everything comfortably worked out before he began, though I doubt it. Perhaps he had a draft completed of something quite conventional before his writer's sense of crisis set in. The point to remember is the same one that Faulkner made to literary critics: they see a finished work and do not dream of the chaos of trial and error and torment from which it has somehow emerged.

No matter what your plan for a novel—and we know Herman was inspired by the account of an actual whaling disaster (the destruction of the ship *Essex* in 1819), and we know how this was a subject, whaling, he could speak of with authority from personal experience abetted by research, and we know he understood as well as the most commercial practitioner of the craft that a writer begins with an advantage who can report on a kind of life or profession out of the ken of the ordinary reader—nevertheless I say that no matter what your plan or inspiration, or trembling recognition for an idea that you know belongs to you, the strange endowment you set loose by the act of writing is never entirely under your control. It cannot be a matter solely of willed expression. Somewhere from the depths of your being you find a voice: it is the first and most mysterious moment of the creative act. There is no book without it. If it takes off, it appears to you to be self-governed. To some degree you will write to find out what you are writing. And you feel no sense of possession for what comes onto the pages— what you experience is a sense of discovery.

So let us propose that having done his first hundred or so pages of almost entirely land-based writing, Melville stopped to read what he had written. What have I got here?—the author's question.

"This Ishmael—he is logorrheic! He is entirely confident of holding my attention whatever he writes about, and whatever he writes about . . . *he takes his time.* With this Ishmael, if I have a hundred or so land-based pages, to keep the proportion of the thing, I will need five hundred at sea. And if the encounter with the whale is my climax, it will need—what?—maybe four hundred and fifty pages of sailing before I find him? Migod."

So there was the problem. His lines were of a texture that could conceivably leave his book wallowing with limp sails in a becalmed narrative sea.

Who knows whether there may have come to Melville one of those terrible writer's moments of despair that can be so useful in fusing, as if with lightning, the book so far with the book to come. In any event, he would for his salvation have to discover that his pages displayed not one but two principles of composition. First, an observance of chronological time, with an identified narrator (Ishmael) and, as in this extended opening or land prelude, a dutiful attendance to the dramatic necessities of conventional fiction—for example, the Elijah-like stranger who issues a cryptic prophecy, the suspenseful nonappearance above deck of Captain Ahab—and surely at this early stage, as we readers can see, the use of humor, good abiding humor of language, and loving character depiction that suggests the shrewdness of a writer who knows his story will end in horror. (Perhaps the least of the things Shakespeare taught Melville was the value of tangential humor to the bloodiest stories: it establishes the hierarchy of human souls that brings the few at the top into tragic distinction.)

All well and good. Melville could project from these traditional storytelling observances a whole series of narrative tropes. Ahab would have to allow the crew the hunting of other whales. So there was that available action. Bad weather and worse could reasonably be invoked—there was that to rely on. As Ahab's maniacal single-mindedness became apparent to the crew, some of them, at least, might contest his authority. (Surely this must have been an attractive option in Melville's mind— a mutinous crew.) There might be the threat of piracy. Finally, other whalers were abroad around the world—they could be hailed and inquired of. As indeed we find, what—eight or nine such encounters? There's the *Albatross,* the *Town-Ho,* the *Virgin,* and on to the *Bachelor,* the *Rachel,* the *Delight*—each ship the occasion for a story and, depending on the usefulness to his passion, a matter for Ahab's approval or rejection. Given this pattern, a habitual recourse of the narrative, we readers today can make a case for *Moby-Dick* as a road novel. (This is not a misnomer when we find through the text repeated equivalences between sea and land, the representation of the one by means of the other. When Ishmael takes up the *Town-Ho* story of Steelkilt and Radney, he steps out of the time of the book and takes us to Peru to tell it, at which point we know he has read *Don Quixote* and perhaps *Jacques the Fatalist.*

But while in these first 105 pages Ishmael's integrity as a narrator is maintained, and the setup for the voyage suggests an assiduous and conventional narrative, there is something else, possibly less visible, a second principle of composition lurking there. It would come to Melville incipiently as a sense of dissatisfaction with his earlier books, and their gift for nautical adventure. While we may know that there is nobody, before or since, who has written better descriptions of the sea and its infinite natures and the wrathful occasions it can deliver, to Melville himself this talent would be of no consequence as he contemplated the requirements of his *Moby-Dick* and felt the aching need to do this book, to bring it to fruition out of the depths of his consciousness—to resolve into a finished visionary work everything he knew.

So he looks again at his Ishmael. And he finds in him the polymath of his dreams.

"Yes, Ishmael tells a chronological story well enough. But look how he does it. He breaks time up into places, things, like someone planting the stones of a mosaic one by one. He has read his Shakespeare. He knows European history. He is conversant with biblical scholarship, philosophy, ancient history, classical myth, English poetry, lands and empires, geography. Why stop there? He can express the latest thinking in geology (he would know about the tectonic plates), the implications of Darwinism, and look, his enlightened cultural anthropology (that I have lifted from *Typee*) grants Queequeg a system of belief finally no more bizarre or less useful than Christendom's.

"I can make this fellow an egregious eavesdropper, so talented as to be able to hear men think, or repeat their privately muttered soliloquies verbatim. See when he finally gives me some action on the schooner from New Bedford to Nantucket, when Queequeg first roughs up a mocking passenger and then saves him from drowning—and this is a nautical adventure despite all—see how when he finally allows a physical action, Ishmael hurries through it to get back to his contemplative ways. My Ishmael was born to be a tactless writer of footnotes—yes, I will make him the inexhaustible author of my water world."

And it is a fact that no sooner are we at sea, in chapter 24, "The Advocate," than Ishmael steps out of time in a big way and gives us the first of his lectures on whaling. Melville's big gamble has begun, *to pass the time by destroying it,* to make a new thing of the novel form by blasting its conventions.

I know this to be true: Herman Melville may have been theologically a skeptic, philosophically an existentialist, personally an Isolato, with a desolation of spirit as deep as any sea dingle—but as a writer he is exuberant.

Even if my scenario is false, and Melville did not need to stop and read what he had written at the point the *Pequod* goes to sea . . . even so, at a hundred or so pages into a book that is working, it begins to give things back to you, it begins to generate itself from itself, a matter, say, of its stem cells differentiating into the total organism. Even with a completed draft of conventional storytelling before him, when the author reads to see what he has done, the lightning strikes early on, and it is the book's beginnings that tell him what finally he must do by way of revision. Thus, from Father Mapple's pulpit like a ship's prow, a rope ladder its means of access, from the story of Jonah as a seaman's sermon, from the Try Pots chowder house, and from the whalebone tiller of the *Pequod,* we derive a landless realm; and by the time much later in the book, when the ship and its crew are four hundred and fifty pages at sea, Ishmael tells us that we—*we*—are still in Noah's flood, that it is eternal, with only the whale able to "spout his frothed defiance to the skies," we need no persuading—the story of Ahab is realized as the universal punishment.

It interests me that Ishmael, who is the source of Melville's inspired subversion of the narrative compact, must therefore be himself badly used by the author. He may be posited as the ungovernable narrator of the novel, but it is Melville who is ungovernable, using Ishmael or dropping him as the mood suits him. Ishmael is treated with great love but scant respect—he is Ishmael all right in being so easily cast out, and if he is called back it is only to be cast out again. I wonder if it was not a private irony of his author that the physically irresolute Ishmael, with roughly the same protoplasm of the Cheshire cat, is the *Pequod*'s sole survivor. I can't help feeling that he would not be so if his continued life was not factually necessary to give voice to the tale—Melville's grudging deference to the simple Job-ic logic of storytelling.

In any event, what Ishmael certainly knows about is whaling—despite his greenhorn status aboard the *Pequod*. He represents himself as having been new to the practice at the time, but by way of compensation, has become well versed in the scientific literature. He likes, like Edgar Allan Poe, to cite extraliterary sources.

I don't know whether Melville read Poe, or what he thought of him, but among Poe's bad writing habits is his attempt to provide authority for the tale he is about to tell by citing presumably factual precedents for it. It's the fiction writer's admission after all that he stands outside the culture of empirical truth. It is a self-defeating move. On occasion, especially at the beginning of *Moby-Dick,* Melville might seem to be doing the same defensive thing—in the very first chapter, "Loomings," he cites men on Manhattan docks fixed in "ocean reveries" and argues the narcissistic attraction of rivers, lakes, and oceans as having to do with water as the "image of the ungraspable phantom of life" to make it more than a personal matter, Ishmael's decision to take to the sea. He cites authorities for the existence of albino whales. And in "The Advocate" chapter, of course, he argues for the social beneficence, the respectability, the grandeur, and so forth of the whaling profession. This sort of nonnarrative case-making to justify the telling of the tale would be as much of a mistake as it is in Poe—if that was as far as Melville took it. But of course, unlike Poe, Melville doesn't stop there: he will load his entire book with time-stopping pedagogy; he will give us essays, trade lore, taxonomies, opinion surveys; he will review the pertinent literature; he will carry on to excess outside the time-driven narrative. It is indisputable in my mind that excess in literature is its own justification. It is a sign of genius, and in this case it turns the world on its head so that just what is a weakness when done in modest proportion is transformative as a consistent recourse and persuades the reader finally into the realm so nakedly proselytized.

And then of course the excess touches every corner, every nook and cranny below deck, every tool and technical fact of the life aboard the *Pequod,* and everything upon it, from Ahab's prosthesis to the gold doubloon he nails upon the mast, from Queequeg's tattoos to the leaking oil barrels in the bowels of the ship. The narrative bounds forward from the discussion of *things.* So finally we look at the details and discover something else: whatever it is, Melville will provide us the meanings to be taken from it. The doubloon upon the mast will be described in such a way—its zodiac signs, its Andean symbols, a tower, a crowing cock, and so forth—as to affirm Ahab's rumination that it is emblematic of an Ahabian universe, the given horror of the half-known life. Queequeg's hieroglyphic tattoos are a "complete theory of the heavens and the earth and mystical treatise on the art of attaining truth; so that Queequeg in his own proper person was a riddle to unfold, a wondrous work in one volume," though he himself could not hope to understand it. And of course, Moby-Dick's color is lifted from him to show "by its indefiniteness" (not a color so much as a visible absence of color) "the heartless voids and immensities of the universe" . . . white being the "colorless, all color of atheism from which we shrink," a "mystical cosmetic" colorless in itself that paints all nature like a "harlot."

Melville's irrepressible urge to make the most of everything suggests the mind of a poet. The significations, the meaningful enlargements he makes of tools, coins, colors, existent facts, are the work of a lyric poet, a maker of metaphorical meanings, for whom unembellished linear narrative is but a pale joy. So I will venture that Melville's solution to his problem is not that of a novelist—it is a poet's solution. *Moby-Dick* can be read as a series of ideas for poems. It is a procession of ideational events. Melville's excesses are not mere pedagogical interruptions of the narrative, nor are they there to provide authority for the tale. They burst from the book as outward flarings or star births, as a kind of cosmology, finally, to imply a multiplicity of universes, one inside another, endlessly, each one of which could have its novel as the sea has this one.

At this point, however, I see that I am in danger of breaking the rules of my engagement with this book. I'm in danger of coming up somewhat off the ground-level observation of the writer at work. Until now I have avoided the autonomy-of-literature argument, or the temptation to speak of the recurrent themes in Melville of the perversities of captainship, the rule of law, the law of men in the universe of a ship, or of Ahab as an archetype, for example, for any of the dictators of recent history. I have not done any of that, but when I talk about the book as a procession of ideational events, or as a metaphoric cosmology, I begin to get nervous.

So I change course here and come about to another claim I can make in my homage to Herman Melville. Many years ago I bought a home in Sag Harbor. Sag Harbor, at the eastern end of Long Island, was once a whaling town, and for some years in the nineteenth century with the whaling industry booming, its denizens had reason to believe that someday, with its deep-water harbor, it would rival New York as a major port. Melville mentions Sag Harbor, gives Queequeg a funny anthropological moment there, and even today it has maintained its village character and is in one sense the town that time has fortunately forgot: the larger Main Street homes, some with their widow's walks built by the whaling captains; the smaller, more modest cottages on the side streets where the ordinary seamen left their families when they went to sea. The cemetery on Jermain Avenue provides gravestone records of the lost captains, the sunken ships, in this most dangerous of trades (so dangerous that it makes Ahab's age the single most unlikely fact of the tale—most captains of the Sag Harbor whaling fleet were quite young, and if they were lucky enough to live to the age of forty or forty-five, they were likely to be burned-out and land-bound forever after—whaling was a young man's get-rich-quick game, in my understanding).

But with Sag Harbor certainly a busy, active whaling community, Melville chose to work his fleet to the north, out of Nantucket. Why?

Now I know the *Essex* hailed from Nantucket, and Melville himself went whaling out of New Bedford right next door and knew the area well. But I would like to believe Melville chose Nantucket because he brilliantly realized that the Quaker speech that predominated there was his means of access, his bridge, to the Elizabethan diction he so exuberantly exercises in his Shakespearean riffs. I will make that my theory of why he chose Nantucket over Sag Harbor, where the Quakers were very small in number and there were no *thees* and *thous* and *dosts* to segue him into the soliloquies and dramatic dialogues that he could not resist. And why would he? I don't know any other writer in history as uncannily able to parody Shakespeare—at moments apt to be equal to him—with his monologues and scenes, but also to so successfully adopt the social structuring of his characters, their hierarchies of rank, comedy, and tragedy, their parallel relationships to those in the master's plays, all of which I assume scholars have annotated in their studies. This is the exuberance in one of its manifestations, the irrepressible love of language that causes Melville to be so eccentric, quirky, and inconstant toward the narrative demands of fiction as to render his book on publication . . . unsaleable.

Certainly *Moby-Dick* is a very *written* book. I'll make a crude distinction here between those writers who make their language visible, who draw attention to it in the act of writing and don't let us forget it—Melville, Joyce, Nabokov in our own time, the song-and-dance men, the strutting dandies of literature—from those magicians of the real who write to make their language invisible, like lit stage scrims that pass us through to the scene behind, so that we see the life they are rendering as if no language is producing it. Tolstoy and Chekhov are in this class, so clearly neither one nor the other method can be said to be *the way*. But the one is definitely more reader-friendly than the other. And Melville, in his journey from *Typee* to *Moby-Dick*, abandons the clear transparent pools of the one for the opaque linguistic seas of the other.

In case my reader is curious, if I aspired to a scholarly position on this occasion, I would invoke Northrop Frye's category of Menippean satire. For after all it can be argued that *Moby-Dick* is that, an Anatomy, a big kitchen sink of a book into which the exuberant author, a writing fool, throws everything he knows, happily changing voice, philosophizing, violating the consistent narrative, dropping in every arcane bit of information he can think of, reworking his research, indulging in parody, unleashing his pure powers of description, so that the real *Moby-Dick* is the voracious maw of the book swallowing the English language.

By way of conclusion I have to admit finally that in interpreting Melville's writing process, perversely applying textual analysis of a sort to read from the finished book what it might have gone through to become itself, I am insisting not so much on the literal truth of my claims but on their validity as another kind of fiction. I confess I have produced here not an essay as much as a story, a parable of the grubbiness and glory of the writer's mind. And I do this mindful that the year 2001 is the hundred and fiftieth anniversary of the publication of this revolutionary novel. Its importance is not negated by the fact that our culture has changed and we no longer hunt the whale as much as we try to save it. In fact, according to newspaper reports, whale watching, not hunting, is now the greatest threat to their well-being, or whale-being. Going out in sightseeing boats to frolic with the whales is a bigger industry now, producing more income than fishing for them, and threatens to disrupt their migratory patterns and thus their organized means of survival. In fact, one can imagine *Moby-Dick* as possibly a prophetic document, if one day a Leviathan rises from the sea in total exasperation at being watched by these alien humans, humans who once at least in hunting whales were marginally in the natural world, but now in only observing them are in that realm no longer, and so rightly destined for the huge open jaw, and the mighty crunch, and the triumphant slap of the horizontal flukes.

But whatever the case, Ernest Hemingway was wrong when he said that modern American literature begins with *Huckleberry Finn.* It begins with *Moby-Dick,* the book that swallowed European civilization whole, and we only are escaped alone on our own shore to tell our tales.

5.

Sam Clemens's Two Boys

SAM CLEMENS WAS THIRTY-SEVEN when he began writing *The Adventures of Tom Sawyer.* He wrote most of it in the space of two summers, 1874 and 1875, devoting the year in between to the business schemes, lectures, writing projects, and domestic and financial matters with which he filled his exuberant life. He spent the summer of 1874 at Quarry Farm, in the countryside above Elmira, New York, with his young wife, Livy Langdon, and their two children, Susy, age two, and Clara, a newborn. Each morning he went off to write in a self-contained study built specially for him, an octagonal room with big windows and panoramic views of the hills and valleys of upstate New York.

Clemens had made himself at home in many parts of the country, any one of which would have contained and nourished another writer for life. A Missourian by birth, he spoke with a slow Southern drawl. But it was out west that he had found fame as a journalist and humorist. His attachment to the state of New York came of his love and courtship of Livy, the daughter of a wealthy Elmira coal mine operator. And now, with his income as a popular American author and lecturer, he was building the grandiose mansion on Farmington Avenue in Hartford,

Connecticut, that would establish him as a literary New Englander, a friend of the famous Beecher family—Harriet, the author of *Uncle Tom's Cabin,* and her brothers and sisters—a close colleague of William Dean Howells, the editor of *The Atlantic Monthly,* and a dinner companion of the elderly Brahmins Emerson and Oliver Wendell Holmes. He was the most peripatetic of authors, unparalleled in restlessness among American writers until then. But the purposive direction of all his travels was up.

The upwardly mobile Clemens was quick to understand both the opportunities and the obligations of his success. Received into the well-to-do Langdon family, he'd muted his views of Christianity and joined their daily prayers. He'd been a bachelor and free-living bohemian until his mid-thirties. As a young man he'd worked on the Mississippi and gone silver prospecting. He'd become a celebrated drinker and cigar smoker in San Francisco saloons. He was the major means of support of his elderly mother, a widowed sister, and a hapless improvident brother. He'd written himself out of genteel Southern poverty and Western frontier gaucherie, but his first fame was as a humorist, a lower-class literary identification that he was still struggling to surmount.

It is the thesis of the most insightful and astute of his biographers, Justin Kaplan, that Sam Clemens's discovery of his "usable past" constituted "the central drama of his mature literary life." *Tom Sawyer,* the first major act of the drama, would come not a moment too soon—the self-attenuation of a literary careerist was as dire in the America of 1874 as it is now. At his writing table in northern New York State, Clemens went back to his beginnings in Hannibal, Missouri, thirty or so years before, a time when "all the summer world was bright and fresh" and "the sun rose upon a tranquil world, and beamed down . . . like a benediction." It was of course a time when the internal conflicts, the stresses and strains, of an invented self complete with its ironic-nostalgic name could hardly have been imagined. In Hannibal, renamed St. Petersburgh in the book, a person needed no education, social position, money, or renown to feel the radiance of heaven. He didn't even need shoes.

Writing without plan from some hastily scribbled notes, Clemens invoked from his past the boy his genius would descry as the carrier of our national soul. He didn't know where Tom Sawyer's adventures would end, thinking at first that they would take him into adulthood. Improvising from one episode to the next, he ran out of inspiration by the end of summer and waited—confident of the empowering past—until it kicked back in a year later. In the months intervening, the book's dimensions managed to clarify themselves in his mind and he decided to leave Tom forever in his boyhood. He wrote to Howells when the book was finished, in July of 1875, "If I went on, now, & took him into manhood, he would just be like all the one-horse men in literature & the reader would conceive a hearty contempt for him." The decision was the right one. But it did not resolve the larger question in his mind of the book's true audience, and both Livy and Howells had to persuade him not to publish it as a work for adults.

The fact is that Clemens's vision of *Tom Sawyer* never quite came into focus. He seemed to want more from the book than it could give—a creative dissatisfaction that would only be resolved with the writing of *Huckleberry Finn*. "Although my book is intended mainly for the entertainment of boys and girls," he wrote in his preface, "I hope it will not be shunned by men and women on that account." The reader today, remembering his own responses to the book as a child, realizes its peculiar duality in adulthood. We can read with a child's eye or an adult's, and with a different focal resolution for each.

Ever since its publication in 1876, children have been able to read *Tom Sawyer* with a sense of recognition for the feelings of childhood truly rendered: how Tom finds solace for his unjust treatment at the hands of Aunt Polly by dreaming of running away; or how he loves Becky Thatcher, the sort of simpering little blond girl all boys love, and how he does the absolutely right thing in lying and taking her punishment in school to protect her; or how he and his friends pretend to be pirates or the Merry Men of Sherwood Forest, accurately interrupting their scenarios with arguments about who plays what part and what everyone must say and how they must fight and when they must die. In addition, child readers recognize as true and reasonable Tom's aversion to soap and water; they share his keen interest in the insect forms of life, and they relish the not always kind attention he pays to dogs and cats. They understand the value he and his friends place on such items as pulled teeth, marbles, tadpoles, pieces of colored glass. And because all children are given to myth and superstition, they take as seriously as he does the proper rituals and necessary incantations for ridding oneself of warts or reclaiming lost possessions by using the divining powers of doodlebugs, as well as the efficacy of various spells, charms, and oaths drawn in blood, although it is sadly possible that children today, divested of their atavistic impulses by television cartoons and computer games, are no longer the natural repositories of such folklore.

There is perhaps less explicit recognition by young readers of the taxonomic world Tom Sawyer lives in, though it accredits and confirms their own: it is the world of two distinct and, for the most part, irreconcilable life forms, the Child and the Adult. As separate species children and adults have separate cultures, which continually clash and cause trouble between them. All of Tom's adventures, from the simply mischievous to the seriously dangerous, arise in the disparity of the two cultures. And because power and authority reside in the Adult, Tom is necessarily a rebel acting in the name of freedom. Thus he is understood not as a bad boy but as a good boy who is amiably, creatively, and as a matter of political principle bad—unlike his half brother Sid, who is that all too recognizable archetype of everyone's childhood, the actually bad boy who appears in the perverse eyesight of adults to be good. (The brothers stand in relation to each other as Tom Jones does to the wretched Blifil in Fielding's great work.)

The moral failures of the adult culture of St. Petersburgh are apparent to the child reader. They range from the imperceptions of the dithering Aunt Polly to the pure evil of Injun Joe. When, with chapter 9, the plot of the book is finally engaged, that is, when Tom and Huckleberry Finn witness the murder at night in the graveyard, the young reader finds everything from then on seriously satisfying, as how could it not be in that it involves the fear of a murderer, the terror of being lost in a cave, the gratification of a court trial that rights an injustice, and the apotheosis of Tom Sawyer as hero of the whole town and possessor of a vast fortune.

Even more satisfying, though not to be consciously admitted as such, is the uniting of the child and adult communities in times of crisis. The whole town turns out along the river when it appears that Tom and Joe Harper have drowned. There is universal mourning. Similarly, when Tom and Becky are feared lost in the cave, the bereavement is understood as the entire community's. The government of the adults is washed away in their tearful expressions of love. And the young reader confirms his own hope that no matter how troubled his relations with his elders may be, beneath all their disapproval is their underlying love for him, constant and steadfast. This is the ultimate subtextual assurance Mark Twain provides his young reader, and it is no small thing for the child who understands, at whatever degree of consciousness, that his own transgressions are never as dire as they seem, and that there is a bond that unites old and young in one moral world in which truth can be realized and forgiveness is always possible.

But what the adult eye reads—ah, that is quite another matter. We open the book now and see Tom as a mysterious fellow, possibly something of an anthropological construct, more a pastiche of boyhood qualities than a boy. He is a collection of traits we recognize as applicable to boyhood, or to American boyhood, all of them brought together and animated by the author's voice. In their encyclopedic accuracy they confer upon Tom an unnatural vividness rather than a human character.

Tom Sawyer is ageless. I don't mean that he is a boy for the ages, although he may be—I mean that he is a boy of no determinable age. When he falls in love he exhibits the behavior of a six-year-old. When he is cunning and manipulative he might be nine or ten. His athleticism places him nearer the age of twelve. And in self-dramatization and insensitivity to all feelings but his own he is unquestionably a teenager. The variety of his moods,

including his deep funks when he feels unloved, his manic ex-
hibitionism, his retributive fantasies, sweeps him up and down
the scale of juvenile thought. The boy doing handstands to im-
press Becky Thatcher is not the same boy who swims across the
river at night from Jackson's Island and, after eavesdropping on
his grief-stricken aunt, elects not to relieve the poor woman's
misery by telling her he is alive. Unlike Lewis Carroll's Alice,
Tom does not have to drink anything to grow taller or shorter.
(I note that the illustrations to the first edition can't seem to decide on Tom's proper height or bulk or the lineaments of his
face.) He's a morally plastic trickster in part derived from the
trickster myths of the African American and Native American
traditions. He may also be the flighty, whimsical, sometimes
kind, sometimes cruel minor sort of deity of classical myth, a
god of mischief, with the capacity to manipulate the actions of
normal human beings, evoke and deflect human emotions, and
in general arrange the course of history to bring honor to himself.

We do not minimize Mark Twain's achievement by noticing,
as adults, some of the means by which it was accomplished. Tom
Sawyer's thought has generative powers. What he fantasizes
often comes to pass. In chapter 3 he receives a cuffing from his
aunt when it is the detestable Sid who has broken the sugar
bowl; in the sulking aftermath, he pictures himself "brought
home from the river, dead, with his curls all wet and his sore
heart at rest. How she [Aunt Polly] would throw herself upon
him, and how her tears would fall like rain, and her lips pray
God to give her back her boy and she would never, never abuse
him any more! But he would lie there . . . and make no sign."
As indeed he doesn't in chapter 15 when he hides under Aunt

Polly's bed, still wet from his night swim, and listens as she weeps and mourns just as he once imagined, and remonstrates with herself in the belief that he has drowned. Tom's fantasies of buried pirate treasure metamorphose into the real buried treasure of Injun Joe. And after Tom and Huck thrill themselves imagining the devilish goings-on in graveyards at midnight in chapter 6, real deviltry arises in front of their eyes in chapter 9, when the grave robbers appear and fight among themselves until one of them is murdered in cold blood. Possibly we are ourselves witness to the author's exploratory method of composition, in which he first conceives of likely things for a boy's mind to imagine, and then decides some of them are too good not to be developed and played out as elements of a plot. In any event a godlike power of realization is conferred upon Tom, as if authorship itself is transferred, and we see a causal connection in what he seriously and intensely imagines and what comes to pass afterward.

Lacking Tom's magical power, the other children in the book tend to be pallidly drawn, with the possible exception of Huck Finn, though he is clearly a preliminary one-dimensional Huck. Becky, we are disappointed to see, is too careless a sketch to be the ideal girl we half fell in love with ourselves as children, and Sid, though showing promise as a villainous Model Boy at the beginning, gradually fades into the background. Mary goes still once Tom's bath is administered, and finds no further reason to be included at all in the life of the village. It is as if the god of mischief sucks up all their vitality into himself—or as if Mark Twain put so much into this free-range American boyhood that he hadn't anything left for the others.

It is the same with the adult parents and authorities in St. Petersburgh, who lack any dimension except the forbearing kindness with which they foolishly greet every outrage perpetrated by the wretched children they have raised. They too are desultory parts of the composition, more impressive really as a village collective or chorus led by Aunt Polly. In some cases the author forgets the names he gives them and supplies them with others. Sometimes he so scants their reactions—as when Tom, the putative Bible-winning scholar, reveals his biblical illiteracy in Sunday school—that he pulls the curtain down over the scene before they can respond at all. And in the climactic return of Tom in time for his own funeral, they fall all over him unbelievably with kisses, and are allowed to ask no questions, let alone to work up an anger, before the chapter comes to its abrupt end.

And yet we indulge the flaws in the composition, perhaps in the author's own spirit of indulgence as he looks down on his lost rural world. In the post-industrial America of today, as in the industrial America of Clemens's own time, *Tom Sawyer* is a work of longing, a version of pastoral, with a built-in entreaty to our critical disbelief. What elicits our tolerance is the voice of the book, which first of all gives candid recognition to the true feelings of its people, and second of all grants them universal amnesty: it is Mark Twain's reigning voice of amused tolerance. Not only are we charmed by its perfect pitch for the American vernacular, but we derive from it a serious self-satisfaction. Its comic rhetoric, its hyperbole, its tongue-in-cheek ennoblement of the actions of a provincial country boy, ask to be read as implicit declaration of a young nation's cultural independence.

There is some indication that the author's own view of his work was less resolute. In his attempt to define what he had done, he claimed *Tom Sawyer* was a kind of hymn. "It is simply a hymn to boyhood," Sam Clemens wrote to William Dean Howells as he struggled with the judgment that his book was more suitable for children than for adults. The claim has a defensive ring to it. Hymns ennoble or idealize life, express its pieties, and are made to be totally proper and appropriate for all ears. In the painful evolution of his creative genius, Clemens was finding it difficult to accept the value of what he had written. He was having to consider the possibility that the voice he had chosen for the book was insufficient to the truth of his usable past. In its celebratory comedy, *The Adventures of Tom Sawyer* might be too forgiving of the racist backwater that had nurtured him. In that sense it purveyed a false sentimentality. If he troubled to draw his boys on a chart, Tom would stand between the Model Boy, Sid, on his right, and the unwashed, unschooled son of a drunkard, Huck Finn, on his left. Tom was a centrist, like Clemens himself, a play rebel who had been welcomed into the bosom of a ruling society he had sallied against. He had been rewarded with every honor it could bestow. It may even have occurred to Clemens that by some perverse act of literary transmutation he had not anticipated, Tom had replaced Sid as the detestable Model Boy.

How could his reviewing eye not wander then to the other one, the skinny, ragged, unredeemable one, swearing to give up all the benefits of civilization if only they would let him alone? What a glorious moment it must have been when the squire of Quarry Farm, the master builder of Hartford's grandest Eastern literary mansion, realized he was in creative contact with a true outsider, the real unrepentant thing, a boy who would never conform, a boy who couldn't read or write but who could turn the tables and speak for the author—a boy who could speak for Sam Clemens from the free territory that had once been his own.

In *Huckleberry Finn,* Sam Clemens releases himself from the tyranny of his Mark Twain stage voice and gives the narration to Tom Sawyer's unredeemable sidekick, Huck. He speaks as a child—and forgoes childish things. And in this rendition of his past his vision of the antebellum South is anything but celebratory. We find not loving adults enduring the mischief of their youngsters but killers, con men, drunks, and thieves. Whereas Tom Sawyer hid out on Jackson's Island because his little girlfriend Becky Thatcher rejected him, Huck flees there, in desperation, to escape the abuses of his alcoholic father, who has threatened to kill him.

Huck links up with Miss Watson's escaped slave Jim, and their adventures rafting down the Mississippi are a variant of the slave narrative. Here the thrown voice of the child comes to genius: Huck, making the socially immoral choice to assist the escape of a slave—someone's rightful property, he thinks—creates in himself an ethically superior morality that he defines as outlaw, and appropriate to such a worthless tramp as he. And Clemens can deal with the monstrous national catastrophe of slaveholding, not head on, in righteousness, in the manner of Harriet Beecher Stowe, but with the sharper stick, the deeper thrust, of irony.

Huck and Jim are survivalists, rafting downstream at night, hiding in the cottonwood banks by day, braving storms, fogs, and steamboat collisions to get Jim to freedom. Civilization here is not, as it is in *Tom Sawyer,* a matter of having your neck washed by a prim maiden aunt. Civilization is buying and selling people, and working them to death. Civilization is a vicious confidence game played on a field of provincial ignorance. Huck, smart and resourceful, is a master of Sawyeresque deception and tale-telling as he confronts the treacherous adults who populate the towns along the river.

And then something terrible happens—terrible for Huck, terrible for American literature. The narrative moves inland, Jim is captured, and Clemens brings back Tom Sawyer. Though the moral mind of the book is Huck's—as Jim's protector, he has been the one to suffer the crisis of his country's conscience—it is given to Tom Sawyer to stage Jim's ultimate escape from the Phelps plantation. Huck, who has been until now our eyes, our voice, moves back to the sidekick role, and the book wallows in foolishness, playing out, long past credibility, Tom's nonsensical, overcomplicated, boy's-book fantasy escape plan. And to render everything completely pointless, it turns out that Jim has been freed legally in the late Miss Watson's will, as Tom has known all along.

Clemens, in his habitual practice of letting a book write itself, stopped work on *Huckleberry Finn,* resumed a couple of years later, put the manuscript away in the drawer again for a few more years, eventually finishing and publishing it eight years, and several other books, after he began. And somewhere along the line he lost his resolve or his way, counting, misguidedly, on the old props of his stagecraft—the mischievous boy and his pranks—to rescue him. They are tawdry here in the real world of Huck and Jim; with the life of Jim at stake, they are cruelly inappropriate.

As a reconstructed Southerner, Sam Clemens was a repository of all the contradictions in his society. Tom's book and Huck's book are conflicting visions of the same past, and at the end of *Huckleberry Finn* one vision prevails, and it is the wrong one. The same thing that made Clemens blow his greatest work generates its troublesome moral conundrum—the depiction of Jim. Clemens loved dialect; he had an ear for it and it came easily to him, so it is Huck Finn who struggles against the white mores of his time to help the black man, Jim, escape from slavery, but it is Huck's progenitor who portrays Jim, in minstrelese, as a gullible black child-man led by white children.

The irony may not be redemptive.

6.

Sinclair Lewis's *Arrowsmith*

Sinclair Lewis, out of Sauk Centre, Minnesota (pop. 2,500), and Yale University, knocked around the world and wrote four irresolute novels before becoming the born-again satirist of *Main Street* (1920) and *Babbitt* (1922). What he realized in these works was an obsessive detestation of American provincial life. And with his inspired invention of George F. Babbitt, the Rotarianized, out-of-shape Realtor, philanderer, and community booster, he proposed a successor to that scamp Tom Sawyer as the carrier of our national soul; Babbitt, philosopher of the commonplace, vacuously professing the business faith that has sucked his soul dry.

Of course, the deadliness of Midwestern provincialism was not Lewis's discovery. Edgar Lee Masters had rung it out in his verses, and Sherwood Anderson was its mournful chronicler in the stories of *Winesburg, Ohio.* Theodore Dreiser had monumentalized its material temptations and spiritual deficiencies in *Sister Carrie.* But none of these artists was as lacking in compassion as Sinclair Lewis. His art was satire. With his comedic gift for exaggeration and his nearly perfect ear for the mindless chatter of social conformity, he found an approving audience in the generations of the Jazz Age for whom a lack of compassion was, like the dry martini, a measure of their liberation.

Sherwood Anderson, all too aware of the potency and popularity of Lewis's novels, wrote: "One comes inevitably to the conclusion that there is a man writing who, wanting passionately to love the life about him, cannot bring himself to do so, and who, wanting perhaps to see beauty descend upon our lives like a rainstorm, has become blind to the minor beauties our lives hold." This view was at the center of the considerable criticism Lewis attracted—that his work was not only savage, but limited, a cartoon rather than a painting, shadowless, without dimension. They asked how any self-respecting novelist could override the ambiguous, the enigmatic, in human life and be as one-sided as this? The answer, which Lewis did not think to provide, is that satire's nature is to be one-sided, contemptuous of ambiguity, and so unfairly selective as to find in the purity of ridicule an inarguable moral truth.

Not that these books didn't have their powerful defenders. H. L. Mencken, himself an urban cosmopolite famously at war with what he called the "booboisie," said of *Babbitt,* "I know of no American novel that more accurately presents the real America. It is a social document of a high order." But it remained for the Europeans to express unqualified approval. H. G. Wells and Somerset Maugham made Lewis an instant peer of the literary realm. And E. M. Forster wrote in a tone of gratitude, "What Mr. Lewis has done for myself and thousands of others is to lodge a piece of a continent in our imagination." That was the truth. Across the Atlantic *Main Street* and *Babbitt* brought news of a spiritual sort that couldn't have been more welcome to a society picking itself up out of the rubble and ruin of the Great War and wanting not at all to ruminate upon the blasted presumptions of superiority of European civilization; so it wasn't the scholarly, stiff-backed, tragic democrat Woodrow Wilson, but the rumpled commercial man Babbitt, sweating out his life of fatuity, who'd provide the conceptual image for the rising behemoth of the New World.

Sinclair Lewis's faculty of self-examination, like that of all writers, was more likely to probe the claims of his critics than the praise of his admirers. In the controversy surrounding *Babbitt,* he defended himself as a "romantic," thus echoing Sherwood Anderson's insight that Lewisian satire was, behind its cynicism, a cry of disillusionment. Expecting his countrymen to be more than they were, looking for a resonant truth and righteousness, Lewis had found an American spiritual life that could elicit from him nothing more than bitter derision.

But with the completion of a book, the writer finds himself further down the road. As he considered what his next novel should be, Lewis could recognize a new figure in his fictional landscape, a romantic composed of his own DNA, a fellow not perfect if he was to be real, but in one way or another disposed to fight his way to a level of existence higher than those around him. He could not be an artist, lest his author be subject to grandiosity, he could not be a priest or a minister, because as a later work, *Elmer Gantry,* would argue, there was dubious salvation in that. Conceivably, he might be a labor leader. But really, the path to a transformed culture was Science, the purest product of the Enlightenment, a calling fresh and clean. Enter Martin Arrowsmith.

———

Arrowsmith is structured as a bildungsroman, a novel of its hero's sentimental education.

The arc of Martin's life rises from the Midwestern village of Elk Mills, where he is found, age thirteen or so, hanging out in the office of an old country doctor and poring over *Gray's Anatomy.* In short order we find him a graduate medical student at the state University of Winnemac. He marries Leora Tozer, and now having a wife to support, he abandons the pure science he has learned at the feet of a renowned but moody bacteriologist, Max Gottlieb, and establishes himself as a country doctor in the small town of Wheatsylvania.

Lacking a bedside manner and the persuasive techniques that would gain the trust of the little farming community, and losing a patient through no fault of his own, he suffers defeat and migrates to the Midwestern city of Nautilus and a position as a public health physician—presumably closer to the ideal of medical research than a family medical practice.

But here too the reality of the job alienates him. The public health officer under whom he works, Dr. Pickerbaugh, knows little science and practices less, but conceives of himself as salesman of the current (and sometimes unfounded) principles of hygiene. Pickerbaugh writes doggerel verse and mounts public-relations events to celebrate clean living. Again Martin finds himself at odds—both with his situation and with the inane society around him.

Rescue seems to come from the Rouncefield Clinic in Chicago, where he gains employment as a pathologist, but once again the surroundings alienate him—Rouncefield being essentially an institution for wealthy surgeons pursuing their fortunes.

Fortunately, Martin has done some research that happens to come to the attention of his cantankerous old professor, Max Gottlieb, now working at the prestigious McGurk Research Institute in New York. Gottlieb, the man who instilled in Martin the love of pure science, the beacon toward which his wavering spirit steers, brings the young man to McGurk, where Martin achieves a professional triumph in the isolation of a bacteriophage that seems effective in the dispatch of pneumonia and plague bacilli. After testing his serum with great therapeutic success, but without true scientific rigor in a Caribbean isle rife with bubonic plague (and losing Leora, his wife, to the plague), Martin returns to New York and abandons his elevated position and a rich new wife, Joyce Lanyon, and the other perks of his newfound scientific celebrity, to go off to the woods with a like-minded colleague, Terry Wickett, and work in a homemade laboratory in pursuit of scientific truth. And so the novel ends as Martin Arrowsmith, having been educated, painfully, in the ways of the world, finally achieves a life that is in accordance with his true self.

But this synopsis suggests that while *Arrowsmith* is structured as a bildungsroman, in spirit it is a morality tale. Oddly, it seems almost to mirror the first novel in the English language, Samuel Richardson's *Pamela,* whose heroine is exercised to defend her virginity against all comers for well over three hundred pages before she is safely married. Martin, for his hundreds of pages, is hard pressed to defend himself from designs not on his person (although his marital fidelity is tested once or twice), but on his integrity of mind. He is plied with money, social acceptance, power, and celebrity, all of which tempt him sorely before he runs off to the woodsy retreat where, as ascetic as any monk, he will live only for his science.

Perhaps intuiting the horrifying lineaments of a morality tale in his projection of the novel, Sinclair Lewis was determined to show that his hero was not heroic. Martin could be likeable, but he must not be consistently admirable. By having Martin stray from the scientific calling at one point or another, and showing him short-tempered as a doctor with patients, or contemptuous toward less gifted colleagues, or by having Martin neglect his wife or insult people who can't understand the value of science research, Lewis was claiming credentials as a true novelist— something his earlier work had not earned for him. And when *Arrowsmith* was published, critics were happy to grant the claim, seeing in the book an artistic maturity, a composition of shadows and dimensions and moral complexity that his out-and-out satires lacked.

It did not hurt that the groundsong or lore of the novel consisted of accurate science reportage. *Arrowsmith* brought to the reading public of the 1920s the news of science. Lewis relied greatly in his preparation of the manuscript on the information and trade gossip supplied by Paul de Kruif, a bacteriologist and immunologist who had worked at the Rockefeller Institute in New York (read McGurk) and was later to achieve fame as a bestselling popular science writer. De Kruif had done the kind of research in immunology attributed in the novel to Arrowsmith. Lewis's biographer, Mark Schorer, tells us that Lewis and de Kruif traveled to the West Indies together (when Lewis decided to make a Caribbean plague the climax of his novel), that the plot was hammered out in conversations between them, and that de Kruif had a contract with Lewis to receive 25 percent of the book's earned royalties.

Nevertheless, coming to this novel some three quarters of a

century after publication, the reader can't help seeing that the truest energies of *Arrowsmith* are those of the satirist, satire and the morality tale being, of course, sides of the same coin. Lewis is as compulsively derisive as ever in his treatment of American society. His irrepressible impulse to ridicule with mimicry emerges certainly in the extended, perhaps overextended, portrayal of Dr. Pickerbaugh, Nautilus's public health official, town booster, bromidic philosopher, and writer of execrable verses—a kind of Babbitt with a medical degree.

Throughout every stage of Martin Arrowsmith's career, and at whatever level of society, he is appalled, alienated, cowed, or simply defeated by the moral shallowness, inanity, stupidity, self-delusion, greed, and hypocrisy of most of the men and women with whom he comes in contact. Very few—his loyal wife, Leora, his mentor, Gottlieb, his pal Terry Wickett—are spared. From the students at Winnemac to Leora's relatives to the country people in Wheatsylvania to the self-important surgeons at the fancy Rouncefield Clinic in Chicago to the fraudulent scientist-politicians at the McGurk Institute in New York, the case is made, as it was in *Babbitt,* of a laughable insufficiency.

The critics of Lewis's time largely failed to note that the Lewisian critique of our culture was no longer restricted to the Midwestern provinces or the commercial men populating them, but bestowed now, generously, over all our geography. As Martin steps up through his life from small town to small city to the big city of Chicago, and finally to the ultimate city of New York, and as he meets people of rising classes of wealth and education, the detestation becomes nationalized and the plague of Sinclair Lewis's curse reaches into every nook and cranny of our social construction.

As the first major American novel to concern itself with the culture of science, *Arrowsmith* seemed a considerable departure for Lewis, a work more substantial than *Babbitt*. Yet Martin Arrowsmith's struggle to be a scientist is a matter of freeing himself from a universe of Babbitts. And though science provides him with his calling, it is at the story's end conflated with living in the wilderness, a vision more of a classic pastoralism than a scientific future.

Lewis's satiric impulse, reflected in his habits of style, prevails, sometimes at the expense of the credibility of the work. Characters speak in riffs of self-damning monologue, the author's most relished device—even Leora, who is thought to be a triumph of characterization (and is in fact quite vulnerable to a feminist critique), speaks in overly self-indicating paragraphs. Both characters and settings are delivered in hasty catalogues and events seem to be sketched on the pages. The overall feel of this bildungsroman is of a running montage, to which even detailed scenes seem subsumed, so that the author's driving intentions are never absent from view.

But withal, Sinclair Lewis, a genius of unappeasable anger and mirthless derision, wanted urgently to shine his light upon us. Who can say it is not illuminating? And who can say of life in America today that the Arrowsmiths aren't few and the Babbitts aren't many? Lewis's fierce moral nature was the source of his greatness, and that is what we close the book on, as we do with any prophet who tells us what we don't want to hear.

7.

Fitzgerald's *Crack-Up*

OF THAT TRIUMVIRATE of hero-novelists who came of age in the 1920s, we may salute the big two-hearted pugilist and stand in awe of the mesmerist from Mississippi, but it's the third one we mourn, the Jazz Age kid, our own Fitzgerald. His was the most natural and unforced of the three authorial voices; his plots required minimal invention; his settings were for the most part the surroundings of his readers. All of that was working the high wire without a net. He lived rashly, susceptible to the worst influences of his time, and lacking any defense against stronger personalities than his own; and when he died, at forty-four, he was generally recognized to have abused his genius as badly as he had his constitution. Yet at his best, in *The Great Gatsby,* much of *Tender Is the Night,* and the incomplete *Last Tycoon,* he wrote nearer to the societal heart than either of his august contemporaries.

The Fitzgerald of *The Crack-Up* is the chastened, mature man, sober, alone, with nothing to lose. He is writing in the Great Depression, but ignoring it except as the turn of events which has, not without justice, dropped him and his Jazz Age ways into the dustbin of history. In a time of breadlines and hobo jungles, and with totalitarian states rising all over Europe, somehow the young man who, one drunken night, leapt into the fountain at the Plaza cannot expect, still, to be everyone's idea of the great American author. But he can reminisce. He can remember the twenties—he can look back on his early success, or the New York of his youthful illusions, or his and his wife's years of sybaritic hotel hoppings, or the circumstances leading to his nervous collapse—and he can render them, bring them back alive for our consideration. Not surprisingly, his tone is elegiac; the sense of a paradise lost infuses every line. But rarely is there a lapse into self-pity. And underneath all is the shrewd writer's assessment of his own rise and fall as a saleable subject. The unstated presumption in *The Crack-Up* (originally published in three installments in *Esquire*) is the author's still lingering celebrity: that golden boy you all remember—see what's become of him.

Whether writing about himself or the changing manners and morals and social dynamics of the time that made him its symbol, Fitzgerald writes with clinical precision. At moments a poetic fever may take hold, when his metaphors stumble over one another in his determination to get through to his magazine audience, but he consistently offers the insights of a first-rate cultural historian. And whatever we say in criticism of him, we find that he has said it first. He is disarmingly confessional about his lack of sustained interest in the universal political crisis of his time, about the squandering of his literary capital in magazine hackwork, about his life as a drunk, about his pathetic need always to prove something to somebody, about his snobberies and prejudices, all held with the passion of an arriviste. Everything we know about him he knows about himself. And it turns out that all along, through all the good times, he was haunted by his inauthenticity—as the young lieutenant in his World War I overseas cap who never got overseas, as well as the urbane young author carried on the shoulders of his generation "who knew less of New York than any reporter of six months standing, and less of its society than any hall-room boy in a Ritz stag line."

Repeatedly he disclaims his role as spokesman and symbol of the Jazz Age, but by reflecting upon it from his chosen distance, he tolls its dreadful excesses in his own life, and so finds its meaning in the body of his wrecked career. There is gallantry in that. We begin to understand our particular affection for this writer. He lacked armor. He did not live in protective seclusion, as did Faulkner. He was not carapaced in self-presentation, as was Hemingway. He jumped right into the foolish heart of everything, as he had into the Plaza fountain. He was intellectually ambitious—but thought fashion was important, gossip, good looks, the company of celebrities. He wrote as a rebel, a sophisticate, an escapee from American provincialism—but was blown away by society like a country bumpkin and went everywhere he was invited. Ambivalently willed, he lived as both particle and wave. "The test of a first-rate intelligence," he wrote, "is the ability to hold two opposed ideas in the mind at the same time, and still retain the ability to function." And while he was at his first-rate quantum best, he used everything he knew of society, as critic, as victim, to compose at least one work, *The Great Gatsby*, that in its few pages arcs the American continent and gives us a perfect structural allegory of our deadly class-ridden longings.

The contemporary reader may have to work to understand the nature of the celebrated crack-up. Fitzgerald tells us that his "nervous reflexes were giving way—too much anger and too many tears." What condition is he describing? A psychotic episode? Depression? A spiritual crisis? There is a muttering resolve in his account of it, a determination at the end to change, to be available no longer to the humiliations that have characterized his fate. "Cave canem," he warns those of us who would come importuning to his door. We have to smile in our sadness for our graying Jazz Age kid. Such bitter resolution is not characteristic of the psychological breakdown, the depleted vitality of the depressive. It is more the angry romantic's expression of inconsolability—in having had an innocence and, having lost it, having to mourn it. That progression of states of the American mind was prevalent once upon a time, but now, after a century of industrialized war and genocide, is itself to be mourned.

8.

Malraux, Hemingway, and the Spanish Civil War

WARS DEMAND NOVELS. The Spanish Civil War, a deadly contest fought from 1936 to 1939, inspired two major works of fiction—André Malraux's *L'Espoir* (translated as *Man's Hope*) and Ernest Hemingway's *For Whom the Bell Tolls.*

Some writers hold ideas for books in their minds for years before they write them. Malraux and Hemingway were writing their novels while the war was still going on. They were men of action who wrote from life. They composed their works out of the places they went and the things they saw. Both were Loyalists, supporters of the Republican government. They came to the war not merely to report on it but to work actively against the Falangists, the fascist insurgent forces of General Francisco Franco.

Malraux arrived in Spain in the summer of 1936. He had earlier arranged for French tanks to be shipped to the Spanish Republicans, before nonintervention policies were put into place by the Western democracies. He traveled about Europe buying airplanes for the Republic as its representative, having understood the importance of an air arm in a war that was becoming progressively mechanized. He then organized the Escadre Espagne, with French, American, English, and German pilots who were veterans of the First World War. Malraux was not himself a pilot but flew with sixty-five missions over Toledo, Madrid, and Guadalajara. After that he came to the United States to raise money for the Loyalist cause. Through all of this he was writing *L'Espoir*. He published it in Paris in 1937, the war in Spain still raging. An English translation was published here by Random House a year later.

Hemingway too was ardently Loyalist, even though as he learned more about the various leftist factions fighting for the Republic against the insurgency, he came to understand that the Communists, who were by far the best organized, had an agenda of their own and could not be trusted, a claim that George Orwell also made and thoroughly documented in his great civil war memoir, *Homage to Catalonia*.

Hemingway covered the war for the North American Newspaper Alliance. He wrote the script for a documentary film, *The Spanish Earth,* to aid the Loyalist cause. He spoke to a left-wing Writers' Congress at Madison Square Garden in New York, an act that put him on J. Edgar Hoover's surveillance list for the rest of his life. All told, he was back and forth to Spain several times during the war, staying famously at the Hotel Florida in Madrid during the insurgent bombardment while he wrote his war play *The Fifth Column.* On his last trip, understanding that with the fall of Barcelona and Madrid the Loyalist cause was lost, he returned to the United States and wrote *For Whom the Bell Tolls,* which was published here in 1940, less than a year after the war had ended.

Hemingway knew Malraux, who also stayed at the Hotel Florida, and did not particularly like him. He called *L'Espoir* a "materpisse." We would not expect Ernest Hemingway to be generous to another writer on the same beat. But the novels these men wrote are not merely the autonomous productions of individual talents; they reflect national dispositions, mythic beliefs, one French, the other American.

Malraux's book begins in the summer of 1936 as Loyalist anarchists are defeating the Falangists in Barcelona. It ends with the Republican victory at Guadalajara in March 1937. But these two victories frame a lost cause. The Republic will go down before the overwhelming Nazi-supplied forces of General Franco. *L'Espoir* is a novel without a plot; it is the war itself that carries us along. And like the war it is filled with battles and human suffering, scenes of brutal fighting, civilian victimization, individual deaths by bullet, by flamethrower, by shrapnel, the action suspended every now and then for serious discussions of ideological matters. The war is described exclusively from the Loyalist point of view, but that doesn't make things less complicated. Fighting for the Republic are left-wing socialists, right-wing socialists, Communists, anarchists, socialist trade unionists, Trotskyists, anarcho-syndicalists, and Republican army officers. As the war progresses, a major theme of the book is that these variegated forces must of necessity organize themselves and suspend their internal disputes if they are to defeat the insurgency. At the beginning the anarchists, implacable foes of the Communists, are fighting for their revolutionary ideals. At the end, they and everyone else are fighting to free Spain of fascism. Malraux, as an airman, writes of the sputtering air war as the Loyalists struggle with old equipment against the superior, more modern, and more numerous aircraft supplied to the insurgents by Hitler and Mussolini. Scenes of aerial war and bombing raids are interspersed with accounts of the ground war. We see inexperienced recruits being installed as "shock troops" on the front lines; we go to hospitals, to executions; we are at the siege of the Alcazar in Toledo; we are under terrible bombardment and then street fighting in Madrid; we watch the Republican stand at the Manzanares River, we follow the long line of fleeing refugees as it is firebombed by the fascists. Above all we are shown how people behave—courageously, or cravenly, or fatalistically—how they are enraged or benumbed in battle. The book is filled with people but very few realized characters—many are no more than names—but they flash into existence momentarily from the dire situations in which they find themselves. Two characters are given repeated attention: one a commander in the air war, the other a leader of ground forces. The airman Magnin survives to fight on; the heroic Hernandez, captured by the fascists, walks to his execution by firing squad though he has an opportunity to escape.

A big, wide-focus, panoramic novel, *L'Espoir* often seems hastily thrown together, with barely believable pretexts for extended political and philosophical conversation. Social theory is assumed to be as essential to a serious novel as it is to a Republican future. But despite the book's weaknesses, what comes through as an ultimate effect is the agony of a country, the terrible chaos and terror of war, the brutality of fascist warfare. *L'Espoir* is in every sense a collectivist novel. If the book has a major character, it is Spain, and the fate of the many people in the book who are given voice or action—soldiers, journalists, doctors, aviators, refugees, peasants, anarchists, Communists, foreign volunteers, children, and insurgent fascists—will be a common fate, the fate that comes down upon an ideologically disfigured country, one in which any idea of a civilized social compact has been ground to dust.

Implicit in the narrative is the presumption of a universal social crisis: if Spain falls under the heel of fascism, what hope is there for the rest of Europe? Malraux claimed he had written a documentary novel. Its dimensions are political. The narrative is urgently voiced, an *engagement*.

European writers have never had as much difficulty as we have with *engagement*. Sartre and Camus, for example, conceived a response to the moral devastation of World War II that included drama, allegory, existential metaphysics, and handing out pamphlets in the street. Except for a few occasions in our history, American writers, less fervent about the political value of art, have been wary of committing their work to a cause. The thirties were one of these exceptional periods—that era of the Great Depression when everyone, left or right, looked for alternatives to the faltering industrial economy. The thirties are now seen as a decade of misfired artistic energy, of duped intellectuals and bad proletarian novels (despite the masters who were writing then—not only Hemingway and Faulkner, but John Dos Passos, Richard Wright, Zora Neale Hurston, Henry Miller). It was the naturalized American poet W. H. Auden who famously said that a writer's politics are more of a danger to him than his cupidity.

If there was a moment when our piety of literary practice was set to harden, it may have been in 1940 with the publication of Hemingway's *For Whom the Bell Tolls.*

Hemingway had published a novel in 1937, *To Have and Have Not,* in which the hero, a smuggler off the Florida coast, came as close as a Hemingway character ever had to articulating a communal sentiment. His name in this book is Harry Morgan, and he's made to say, "A man alone ain't got no bloody fucking chance." This was a radical insight coming from this younger sibling of the romantically self-involved heroes of the earlier 1920s novels.

With Hemingway's steep involvement in the Spanish Republican cause, it would have seemed likely to some critics that his next novel would go even further in a communal direction. He knew the situation in Spain for what it was—an assault by a religiously inflamed coalition of royalists, priests, and general officers seeking to overthrow a democratically elected government that had proposed to lift the Spanish people out of feudal poverty. Like most everyone else, he also understood that a Falangist victory in Spain would lead to a larger war on behalf of European state fascism. He had seen the hostilities firsthand; he was more worldly and more in touch with things than his co-generationists Faulkner or Fitzgerald. But when we read *For Whom the Bell Tolls,* we discover that a man alone may have no bloody fucking chance but it can be very beautiful that he hasn't.

The Hemingway hero, here named Robert Jordan, is a young American volunteer on the Loyalist side, a demolitions expert, a sapper, who has come alone to the mountains northwest of Madrid, behind enemy lines, to blow a bridge held by the Falangists. His mission is understood to be crucial to a Republican offensive. The novel covers just three days in time. And there are five extremely well-drawn main characters in Jordan and the members of the guerrilla peasant band who are enlisted to help him—Pablo, their titular leader; his wife, Pilar, who is the stronger of the two and takes over the leadership of the band when Pablo indicates his reluctance to assist Jordan; Maria, a beautiful young woman whom Pilar has saved, and with whom Jordan falls in love; and Anselm, an old man who is loyal to the Republican cause but a pacifist at heart, a humanitarian who believes that the enemy rank and file they fight are simple men, as he is. Jordan and Maria fall in love; Pablo seems to desert but returns and regains his courage.

Jordan has reason to believe the Republican attack plans have leaked to the Falangists, and he sends a younger member of the guerrilla band back to his headquarters requesting that the mission be canceled. But the message arrives too late and Jordan is ordered to go on as planned. When Jordan blows the bridge, he is wounded in the action. He sends the guerrillas away, protecting their escape by covering a defile with a submachine gun as he awaits the arrival of the enemy force and his own impending death.

A far more brilliant and technically adroit writer than Malraux, Hemingway portrays the big war symbolically with his little one. He would observe the unities of time and place, though he cannot quite manage that: two inserted dramatic episodes, the bombing of a mountain stronghold of another guerrilla leader known as El Sordo, but especially the guerrilla woman Pilar's account of when the peasants in her village brutally abused and killed their fascist neighbors—a story she tells at great length—finally show the strain of his formalism.

Implanting *For Whom the Bell Tolls* in a discrete geography and in measured time were finally dramatic strategies that were not capacious enough for its subject. While it is true that we extrapolate some of the political complexities of the war in Hemingway's comments about the leadership of the Loyalists, portrayed as cynical and careless of the ideals of the ground forces they lead (particularly in flashback scenes as Jordan recalls his evenings in Madrid at Gaylord's hotel), and though he is sharper than Malraux in his perception of the Russian Communist leadership as essentially treacherous (Malraux, as more of a revolutionary mystic, would seem at points to justify Stalinist tactics on the grounds of their efficacy), and while he grants the average enemy soldier the same simple humanity as his own side's and crosses political lines to defame the Spanish character in general as given to mercurial feelings and a penchant for betrayal—for all of these nuances, Hemingway's novel is finally a romance. Robert Jordan ends up dying alone, heroically, having taken over the leadership of the partisan band he's joined and sent them away to live on, his own code of honor seeming to be the only enduring value of the civil war of the Spanish people. This most expatriate of American writers, whose major work was to be set in Europe, was, morally speaking, an isolationist. War is the means by which one's cultivated individualism can be raised to the heroic. And therefore, never send to ask for whom the bell tolls; it tolls so that I can be me.

Where Malraux's novel emphasizes experience in such a crisis as collective, Hemingway's delineates such experience as a test of a single person's moral stature. Malraux's characters are barely realized as the action flows through them to give them their momentary animation; Hemingway's characters are bigger than the war, their wills are dominant, and the interactions among them occur mostly in a setting—a secret cave and the woods around—that is as closed and as confining as a drawing room in Jane Austen. There is de facto political meaning to be derived when a writer creates from the momentous materials of the Spanish Civil War a novel of sensibility.

Hemingway was hardly inactive in his efforts on behalf of the Loyalists. He was brave and put his life in harm's way. But his *engagement* was personal; as an artist he drew the line. So there were two Hemingways at the war: the writer was there to gather the materials for a book. I note that he makes Robert Jordan a college professor of Spanish who, with no identifiable political sponsorship, has come to fight from a love of Spain and her culture. Hemingway's problem—self-created, like most writers' problems—was to get Robert Jordan to Spain in a way that didn't define him as most young American volunteers who came to Spain to fight for the Republic were defined—not only as antifascists, the broadest category that could contain them, but as communists or socialists of one variety or another. Because, in fact, that's what they were. They were organized as the Abraham Lincoln Battalion. A majority of them were American Communist Party members or recruits of the Young Communist League, although the volunteers included socialists and registered Democrats. Some 40 percent were Jewish, a good many I suspect devolved from the non-programmatic tradition of radical Jewish humanism. A hundred or so were black. Most of them were students or seamen. And out of the three thousand or so total volunteers, some eighteen hundred lost their lives.

Casting Robert Jordan as a Spanish professor and as a lone

guerrilla, Hemingway proposed the Spanish Civil War as a test of one's self-reliance, not only in the face of an armed enemy, and not only in the bosom of a native population that could not entirely be trusted to act properly in the cause of its own freedom, but as one apart from the numbers of young radicals of dubious background who comprised the majority of American idealists who came to fight on the Loyalist side. Robert Jordan might have been antifascist, but Hemingway didn't want him to be a *premature* antifascist.

We can easily discern *L'Espoir* as a political novel—a novel that addresses the political nature of historical events, that subjugates its characters to forces beyond their control, and that casts its storied conflicts in ideological terms. Malraux reiterates the eternal attention of the French writer to the materials of history; these are to be analyzed and are to serve as instruction. His novel reflects his nation's belief in the supreme value of the social intellect.

Hemingway is a magnificent artist whose work will outlast Malraux's because it more clearly honors the literary act for its intrinsic value. But he too has written a political novel expressive of a national myth. His novel as conceived happens to accord perfectly with the American abhorrence for political theorizing, big systematic solutions, and utopian dreams. His aesthetic places the artist's idea of himself centrally in the American heartland. The notion that we are the self-reliant independent entrepreneurs of ourselves is a national heritage. Working people in the United States, unlike their European counterparts, refuse to identify themselves as a class. They tend to define themselves not by their work but by what they own from their work, or by their ethnic background, or their social activities. For the independent entrepreneur of himself there can be upward mobility, at least across generations, and there is the road—he can hit the road when things go bad, pull up stakes and move on. All this, including the writer's idea of what he can allow in his art and what he cannot, celebrates our great operative myth of rugged individualism. It is the myth tied to the American historical accomplishment. It is a constituent of our freedom. Given a nation of self-reliers, you can make the case for American exceptionalism.

The economic metaphor for this myth is the "free market." In politics it is a dependable source of a candidate's appeal. Presidential candidates tend to run as outsiders even though they may come from well-established political dynasties. The current president has no patience for the United Nations, wants to go it alone, and has gone to war alone. He advertises himself as the rugged individualist par excellence. Of course, none of this cynical exploitation of a means of our national identity is Hemingway's responsibility. But it is at least possible that his long-standing popularity with the public and among young writers might be due in part to his service on behalf of a prevailing societal myth. Entrepreneurial self-reliance had come in for some rough treatment from Melville in *Moby-Dick,* and from Dreiser in *Sister Carrie,* and from Fitzgerald in *The Great Gatsby,* but Hemingway found its most romantic face. Distrust of society, a principled loneliness, have been preponderant motifs in our fiction ever since Robert Jordan withdrew from hope for his life and for the antifascist cause and waited for death as he looked out over the barrel of his machine gun on the last page of *For Whom the Bell Tolls.*

9.

Dos Passos: *U.S.A.*

GIVEN NEITHER TO HE-MAN AESTHETICS, like Hemingway, nor to the romance of self-destruction, like Fitzgerald, John Dos Passos, their friend and contemporary—he was born in 1896— was a modest, self-effacing person, an inveterate wanderer who liked to hike through foreign places and sit down for a drink with strangers and listen to their stories. He saw literature as reportage. He admired the plain style of Defoe, and he read Thackeray's *Vanity Fair,* subtitled *A Novel Without a Hero,* all his life.

Dos Passos was born wandering, living out his lonely childhood with his unmarried mother, Lucy Madison, as she toured the European capitals to avoid scandal, while in the United States, his father, John R. Dos Passos, an eminent corporate lawyer and lobbyist, waited for his invalided first wife to die. When that event came about in 1910, the mother, the father, and the boy, a strongly loving triad, were finally able to constitute themselves as a family. But the isolation of his early life left Dos Passos psychologically detached, with the feelings of a perpetual outsider.

The outside, of course, is a position of advantage for a writer. Reportage from the outside, and slightly above, is the working viewpoint of Dos Passos's masterpiece, *U.S.A.* It is a nice irony that not the era's big literary personalities, but this quiet, inhibited young man, would produce the most vaultingly ambitious novel of all—a twelve-hundred-page chronicle of the historic and spiritual life of an entire country in the first three decades of the twentieth century. Not for him the portrait of a gangster, however metaphorically shimmering, nor even the group portrait of a lost generation: Dos Passos goes wide—from the American incursion in the Philippines to the beginning of the talkies, from coast to coast and class to class. *U.S.A.* is the novel as mural, with society's heroes standing out from the flames of history while the small-figured masses toil at their feet.

In fact, the peripatetic Dos Passos landed one day in Mexico City and was much taken with the murals of Diego Rivera colorfully spreading, story after story, up the courtyard walls of the Secretariat of Education. In later years he indicated also his love of thirteenth- and fourteenth-century European tableaux—those with the saints painted big and the ordinary people painted small, filling up the background.

He published the first installment of *U.S.A.*, *The 42nd Parallel*, in 1930, having realized early on that what he was doing could not be contained in one volume. *1919* followed two years later, and the final volume, *The Big Money,* was published in 1936. He could have gone on—he had endless resources for the thing, having picked up its rhythm and much of the material from his own ambulating life. He'd gone up from Baltimore to Harvard, where he read, and was impressed by, the Imagist poets—Pound, Amy Lowell, Carl Sandburg. He also made his acquaintance with the work of James Joyce, the twentieth-century writer who, though hardly given to English plain speech, would have the most enduring influence on him. After Harvard he went back to his wandering, spending a year in Spain and studying architecture. But World War I was just over the border, and in 1916 he volunteered to drive for the Norton-Harjes Ambulance Corps, the same organization for which Hemingway and e. e. cummings drove. He served in France and Italy, and then with the entry of America into the conflict he enlisted in the American Expeditionary Force and, all told, got as much of a dose of modern war as he would need for the inspiration to portray its soldier-victims in his first novel, *Three Soldiers* (1921).

The reticent writer was always disposed to the action. In the postwar twenties, he managed time and again to place himself in history's hot spots—whether the literary scene in New York and Paris, revolutionary Mexico after the death of Emiliano Zapata, the newly Communist Soviet Union, or the nativist city of Boston, where he marched for the two imprisoned and condemned immigrant anarchists Sacco and Vanzetti.

He was writing all the time, of course. He published *Rosinante to the Road Again* (1922), a book of essays about Spain; *Manhattan Transfer* (1925), a dark impressionist portrait of New York and a technical precursor of the *U.S.A.* novels; and pieces in *New Masses, The Dial, The Nation,* and *The New Republic* attesting to his leftist sensibility. He was a diarist and kept up an active correspondence with a variety of colleagues including Edmund Wilson, Malcolm Cowley, and Ernest Hemingway—all of them worried in the world, all of them news junkies arguing politics and entangling themselves in the crises of civilization.

Not until the Spanish Civil War would the profound difference between Dos Passos's humanist ideals and the doctrinaire idealism of many of his contemporaries become clear: the visible moment of separation seems to have occurred with the execution in Valencia of his friend José Robles, a Republican, by a Communist firing squad.

In his later life Dos Passos was as archly conservative as he had been radical. What remained constant, like a moral compass course that never veered, was his despair of the fate of the single human being bent into service of the institutions of modern industrial society, whatever those institutions might be.

In fact, the pervading vision of *U.S.A.* is of people dominated by institutions, which is to say trapped in history. The novel is without a hero. We are given narratives of the lives of a dozen men and women—Joe Williams, a seaman; Mac, a typesetter; J. Ward Moorehouse, a public relations man; Eleanor Stoddard, a stage designer; Dick Savage, a Harvard graduate and World War I ambulance driver; Charley Anderson, a wartime air ace and inventor; Margo Dowling, an actress; Ben Compton, a union organizer; and so on—and watch three decades pass through them as they reach their prime and then age and flounder, either to die or simply to disappear or, with one or two exceptions, to end in moral defeat. Living below the headlines, they're presented as ordinaries: their lives can intersect, they can sometimes be charming or sympathetic, but they are always seen from above, as in satire, and all their irresolution, self-deceit, and haplessness, and their failure to find empowerment in love or social rebellion, is unconsoled by the moral structure of a plot. *U.S.A.* has no plot, only the movement forward of its multiple narratives under the presiding circumstances of history.

The circumstances themselves are occasionally flashed to us

by means of the so-called "Newsreels" that interrupt the text with actual headlines from newspapers of the time, fragments of news stories, advertising slogans, and popular song lyrics all popping up in rat-a-tat fashion like momentary garish illuminations, as from fireworks, of the American landscape.

Early readers were dazzled, as they should have been, by these collages. But Dos Passos does not stop there. A third mode is the minute biography, the periodic insertion into the text of highly editorialized brief lives of some of the paramount figures of each of the decades he covers—including Eugene Debs, William Jennings Bryan, Andrew Carnegie, Thomas Edison, John Reed, J. P. Morgan, Teddy Roosevelt, Woodrow Wilson, the Wright brothers, Henry Ford, Isadora Duncan, and William Randolph Hearst—the secular saints of the Dos Passos tableau, often mocked, sometimes mourned, but in any event drawn big. Unlike the lives of his fictional characters, which flow incessantly—the breathless author saying "and then this happened and then that happened"—the biographies stand as firm in his annunciation as historical markers.

Through the fourth major mode of address of the book, those Joycean passages under the heading "The Camera Eye," Dos Passos records his own nameless life of sensations beginning with his early boyhood. These are perhaps the most enigmatic interludes. Like the Newsreels and brief biographies, they give a topographical dimension to the text, as if points in the main narrative were being held under a higher lens magnification. They also implicate the narrator in the narrative, serving to underscore his moral commitment to the act of writing. But with his characteristic self-denigration, Dos Passos once justified these sections to an interviewer as planned lapses into "the subjective," a way of keeping this terrible contaminant out of the rest of the manuscript.

Here we should remember D. H. Lawrence's warning to trust not the writer but the book. As with Dos Passos's self-effacement, his objectivity, which is the literary form of self-effacement, masks an imperial intelligence, an acerbic wit, a great anger, and, above all, the audacity to write a novel that breathes in the excitements of all the revolutionary art of the early twentieth century—whether Joyce's compound word streams or Rivera's proletarian murals or D. W. Griffith's and Sergei Eisenstein's film montages.

The stature of *U.S.A.* was immediately recognized by the critics of the day. By the time of its publication as a completed one-volume trilogy in 1938, the novel was generally regarded as a major achievement, although displaying the characteristics of a highly controlled vision. Malcolm Cowley thought of it as a "collectivist novel" perversely lacking the celebrations of common humanity that would be expected from a collectivist novel. Edmund Wilson wondered why every one of the ordinary characters of the book went down to failure, why nobody took root, raised a family, established a worthwhile career, or found any of the satisfactions that were undeniably visible in actual middle-class American life. Others objected to the characters' lack of ideas, Dos Passos's refusal to give them any consequential thought or reflection not connected with their appetites. And it is true that these are beings occupied almost entirely with their sensations and plagued by their longings, given mightily to drinking and fornication while their flimsy thought provides no anchor against the drift of their lives.

But for Jean-Paul Sartre, writing in 1938, it was exactly in the novel's refusal to redeem its characters that he found its greatness. Their lives are reported, their feelings and utterances put forth, says Sartre, in the style of a "statement to the press." And we the readers accumulate endless catalogues of individual sensory adventures, from the outside, right up to the moment the character disappears or dies—and is dissolved in the collective consciousness. And to what purpose all those feelings, all that adventure? What is the individual life against history? "The pressure exerted by a gas on the walls of its container does not depend upon the individual histories of the molecules composing it," says the French existentialist philosopher.

But *U.S.A.* is an American novel after all, and we recognize the Americanness of the characters. They really do have a national specificity. In fact, the reader now, almost a century farther along, cannot help remarking how current Dos Passos's characters are, how we could run into Margo Dowling or Ward Moorehouse or Charley Anderson today and recognize any one of them, and how they would fit right in without any trouble. How they do fit in. *U.S.A.* is a useful book to us because it is far-seeing. It seems angrier and at the same time more hopeful than it might have seemed in its time. A moral demand is implicit in its pages. Dos Passos says in his prologue that, above all, "*U.S.A.* is the speech of the people." He heard our voice and recorded it, and we play it now for our solemn contemplation.

10.

Harpo

LIKE ALL CITY CHILDREN of my generation I revered the Marx Brothers. I don't recall bothering to understand why they were so funny, but I looked forward to each of their movies for what I knew would happen: they would dismantle any society in which they found themselves. Everywhere they went they brought chaos and confusion. Nothing could stop them.

Groucho, Chico, and Harpo may not have been the only comedians to outrage propriety, violate custom, and make a shambles of the hope of human dignity, but they disdained the dramatized self-usage of a Keaton or a W. C. Fields, offering instead the brazen assertion of themselves as Marx brothers no matter what names were assigned to them by their screenwriters. Always they stood outside the milieu of their movies, heaping verbal or physical abuse on any character actor who had the misfortune to serve as their foil. They were unremitting surrealists. Even their musical interludes—Chico at his piano, Harpo at his harp—had no discernible dramatic justification. What made them the most radical of their profession was that their comedy, unmediated by anything like normal sentiment, went to the root of the vital social pretense that life is purposeful and the universe subject to reason.

Had we not had the Marx Brothers at the opera, at the races, aboard ship, or at war, I think there would have been perhaps less understanding from us in later life of such exemplars of modernism as Giorgio de Chirico, Marc Chagall, Luis Buñuel, and Samuel Beckett.

Though Zeppo Marx occasionally appeared as a straight man, as far as we children were concerned, there were just the three brothers. Chico we liked the least—perhaps because he was the least funny, or his characterization was thinnest, or because we detected something slipshod or false in his performances. Groucho, we acknowledged, was the wit. He had the words, he sang the songs, and was usually conniver of the plot and organizer of things (though in the true and anarchic spirit of the Marx Brothers, their alliances were subject to instant revision and the other two as often as not might make him the victim of their slapstick). But there were moments when we felt menaced by Groucho, as if there was some darkness in him, or some inadvertent revelation of the sadistic lineaments of adulthood that was perhaps premonitory of our own darkness of spirit as when we laughed guiltily at his ritual abasement of the statuesque, maternal Margaret Dumont.

Where Harpo was concerned, there were no reservations. He was our favorite. He was the Marx brother we truly loved. Groucho may have had command of the language, and Chico as well, under the constraints of his oddly chosen Italian accent, but Harpo, in speaking not at all, was our spokesman.

Harpo communicated by putting his knuckles to his teeth and whistling, or by honking the car horn he pulled from his voluminous pockets. When the situation was dire he could warn Chico with a charade. When a pretty girl walked by, his remarkably pliant face—the glazed-over eyes, the dropped jaw—told us everything we needed to know in that split second before he took up the chase. Speechless, he was the purest clown of the three. His wig, his crushed top hat, and those depthless pockets that gave forth scissors, saws, lighted lamps, working telephones, kitchen utensils, and dead chickens, were the trappings of a genius kid. We too were sometimes the proud possessors of what the world thought of as junk. We too had that swiftness of foot that would allow us to chase girls and manage never to catch them. We too understood everything there was to know about the adult world . . . but said nothing.

We loved Harpo because instinctively we knew he was one of us. But we couldn't have understood that his own life as a child might have been the reason for our recognition. In fact, the creative depth of his clowning had to have come from something more profoundly ingrained in his nature than his adult experience in the theater as one of the Marx Brothers about to hit it big in Hollywood. It is impossible to believe that the first time Harpo hung his knee on the hand of the startled distinguished actor standing next to him, that it was a planned routine. It had to have been the inspired improvisation of someone who had grown up in the street, as Harpo did in the streets of New York in the raucous 1890s, where survival depended on one's precise stance toward authority. The Marx Brothers' movies are all about outwitting authority. But apparently it was the gleeful Harpo, the family's street urchin so constantly in its presence, who learned to hustle it with a goofy leer, and make it the inadvertent minion of his own surreal authority.

Handing your leg to a distinguished person is a not inconceivable metaphor for someone, like Harpo, who as a kid had only one ice skate to skate on. Making a comic routine out of a wealth of found objects in your pockets has a certain resonance if as a boy you sustained yourself by selling to junk dealers the treasures you found in the street or stole from moving vans.

The world young Harpo had to outwit included not only cops, truant officers, and neighborhood toughs, but also his family's impoverishment and a degree of distraction from his loving parents that allowed him to drop out of school in the second grade. He had to outwit the New York of his day that gave to such children of immigrants as Adolph "Harpo" Marx a tenement airshaft in which to hang his Christmas stocking, and the luxury of attending New York Giants baseball games on a hill outside the ballpark from which he could see only the left fielder.

The reader will find no self-pity in Harpo's memories—they are recounted with the humor of someone who long ago arose from them into a triumphant professional life. But Harpo's stories make it clear that in his critical early years the world never quite assembled itself from the fractured understandings of his experience into anything comfortably ordinary or rational. The city of New York was in that day an atonality of immigrant cultures, with adjoining blocks ringing with different languages. Children who wandered into streets not their own were routinely mugged. The homes of the rich abutted the homes of the poor. Brewery owners stood in for aristocracy as their liveried carriages clattered over the cobblestones past the awed gaze of urchins. New York was a raucous municipal democracy in which citizenship was not a requirement for voting. The most exciting holiday of the year was not Christmas but Election

Day, because it was celebrated by the lighting of enormous bon-
fires in the middle of every street in every neighborhood.

A collage of disparate, violently-yoked-together elements,
New York was the surreal composition of a mad artist. Perhaps
in some instinctive way Adolph Marx understood that and it led
to his deliverance. Or else why, as Harpo, would he remember
so fondly . . . his watch with no hands . . . his lone ice
skate . . . the wedge of outfield grass in the Polo Grounds . . . or
the old warped harp that had been his grandmother's, standing
in a corner as if waiting for him?

II.

Heinrich von Kleist

AMPHITRYON, THE GREAT THEBAN COMMANDER, returns from war to find his palace, and his wife, in the possession of an imposturing double. Struggling to reclaim his identity, he rages against the impostor as a

> . . . lying spirit up from hell, who wants
> Me out of Thebes, and out of my wife's heart,
> Out of the world's remembrance, if he could,
> Out of the fortress of my consciousness.

A Kleist play may be set in ancient Greece, in Holland, or in seventeenth-century Prussia, but the fortress of consciousness is where the action occurs; inevitably, the walls are breached and the ramparts overrun. We feel Kleist's heroes and heroines are entitled to the trances, fainting fits, and visions to which they are continually subject, for in his universe everything is simultaneously its opposite—a man's identity is not his own, love is murder, military heroism is treason, the sitting judge is the guilty party. Kleisteans struggle monumentally with their perceptions; something else than what they expected is happening to them. That may be why, almost two centuries after these plays were written, we find them disturbingly current. In our century we acknowledge the genius of Isaac Newton but know that the universe we live in is, irrevocably, Einstein's. Similarly we give homage to Goethe but recognize ourselves as denizens of Kleist. No wonder Franz Kafka loved this writer and read him aloud to friends.

Perhaps the most stunning feature of Kleist's work is its faculty of narrative advance. This is as true of his plays as it is of his prose. No matter what he writes for the stage—rustic comedy, high tragedy—the tempo of consequential event is unfailing, the action is headlong and unceasingly generative. Typically, some sort of infernal proposition launches the work, some disorder of the world's logic: it powers its way through the lives of the characters as a demonic animation that possesses them and, like the god Jupiter who has come to earth in the form of Amphitryon, appropriates their very being.

In *Prince Frederick of Homburg,* for example, the young Prince wins the day against the Swedes at Fehrbellin, but his triumph comes of a reckless disregard of his battlefield orders from the chief of state, the Elector of Brandenburg. So two Prussian values—personal courage and military obedience—are mounted in one self-contradictory event. The Elector accepts the Prince's victory and sentences him to death. The heroic Prince expresses the most abject cowardice as he pleads for his life—even to the point of bartering his fiancée's love for it. Then he finds a stoic, statist rationalization for his death, and thereby wins a last-minute reprieve.

In Kleist things change and they change fast. The protagonist's mind undergoes an alternation of ecstasies and despairs as it spins on the axis of Kleistean paradox. *Penthesilea* begins with the young warrior queen of the Amazons sweeping down indiscriminately on Greeks and Trojans alike, disrupting their warfare with a furious campaign. Why? She wants the great Achilles as a prize of war. He allows himself to be taken, whereupon her ferocity gives way to her love and she becomes the most demure of women and agrees to follow him. Has she won Achilles or has he won her? Rebuked by the High Priestess of her nation, Penthesilea recovers her sense of honor. She cannot reconcile her feelings, she can only suffer them in turn. This is not true of Achilles, who is pragmatic. He makes the mistake of wooing her in the language of war. Penthesilea kills him and falls on his body like a ravening dog.

The excess of self, the irrepressible force of individual love and passion and desire, is always present in Kleist, and always portrayed as a threat to the ruling order. Even in the earliest of his plays, the genuinely farcical *Broken Pitcher,* in which the lascivious and bumbling Judge Adam must hear a case in which his own sexual scandals come to light, there is a district examining judge to uphold the claims of society. We begin to perceive the structure of Kleist's imagination as a repertory company of players whose costumes and titles and gender change from work to work, but who stand in fixed relation to one another and to the argument. Amphitryon, Prince Frederick, the beautiful Queen Penthesilea, and even the randy Judge Adam all hold high rank in their respective societies and command a following. Typically, one of the followers is a trusted aide or servant who will attempt to intercede and mediate in a voice of practicality and reason when the problem arises. The problem arises when someone of even higher rank than the hero or heroine, someone older who is himself, or representatively, the source of all rank and position—Jupiter, or the Elector of Brandenburg, or the High Priestess of Diana, or District Judge Walter—moves to impose the will or judgment of God or state.

One way or another God and state always win in the end. This outcome is perhaps most troublesome to us in *Prince Frederick of Homburg.* Here Kleist seems clearly to be arguing the virtue in the submission of the individual to totalitarian rule—Frederick, after all, affirms the justice of his own death sentence. And the end of the play seems celebratory. But is it? The constant shifting of Prince Frederick's fortunes, and with it his mind's conditioning, proposes itself as Kleist's real vision. If there is any rule of life, he seems to say, it is volatility. What has the Prince undergone if not a form of brainwashing? Is the state anything more than his delusion? Kleist's Germanic passion was for an objective order or truth, a system of certainty that could not be sabotaged by his thought. This passion was never satisfied. And so, at the moments of resolution in his plays, odd or ambiguous things happen, irrepressibly, as if to suggest the lie involved even in bringing a piece of work to conclusion. "No, tell me," says the Prince, his life and love and glory given back to him, "is it a dream?" He may here be using a metaphor for incredible happiness. Or he may be suggesting life's ephemeral insubstance. In any event, he is assured that a dream is what it is, and that is the way the play ends.

Even more ambiguous is the ending of the comedy *Amphitryon.* At the very moment of happy resolution—Amphitryon's soul reseated, his rights and privileges returned by the god Jupiter—his wife, Alcmena, lets out a guttural cry of despair. It is the last word of the play, the woman's realization that she has

had the love of a god, but from now on will have only Amphitryon.

In the embattled fortress of consciousness there is no end to
warfare, only the incessant flow of the contending forces of sub-
jectivity as they advance and fall back, occupy or give up the
blasted structure. Kleist's dramas are beautifully constructed,
each informed by a shrewd stagecraft and skillful use of convention. (Even his employment of props—a lady's glove, the bent
plume of a helmet, a bloodied arrow, a broken pitcher—is con-
summate.) If you were preparing any of these works for stage
production you would be hard pressed to find a scene, or even a
passage, that is extraneous—so elegantly are they put together.
But it is a final Kleistean irony that the overwhelming sense of
his plays is of immense disorder, teeming madness, an infernally
wild fluctuation of feeling and event. Kleist makes excessive demands on his characters and gives them excessive responses that
call up his greatest powers as a metaphorist and dramatic poet.
He leaves us with a body of dramatic work that, though small
and neatly made, seems to enlarge and grow jagged in our contemplation.

12.

Arthur Miller

IN AN ARTHUR MILLER PLAY there is always a day of reckoning: it arrives at that point in a man's life when truth bursts through his self-delusion and he is overwhelmed. The means by which he has failed himself and others is given full expression and the cost is borne. As Miller himself has said, this is the classical Greek concept of theater: "I come out of that tradition . . . where the past is the burden of man and it's got to be placed on the stage so that he can grapple with it . . . it's the story of how the birds come home to roost. Every play."

Yet within the rigors of that tradition Miller has depicted an astonishing variety of lives, of different classes and from different periods of our history. He has provided us a body of work that transcends its undeniable theatricality, its skillful applications of suspense and conflict, its glory in characterization and play of language, to implicate us, the audience, in its action to a degree achieved by perhaps no other American playwright. It is not merely good storytelling that yanks us up there onstage with the salesman Willy Loman or the longshoreman Eddie Carbone or Lyman Felt, the wealthy businessman of *The Ride Down Mt. Morgan* (1991), but the author's evidentiary case for the moral immensity of human life.

Miller deplores the label of *naturalist* which has stuck to him since his early drama *All My Sons* (1947), his one venture in a well-made, fourth-wall play in the manner of Ibsen. He is right about that. Even the subsequent *Death of a Salesman* (1949), a poetically conceived play of multiple realities imposed one upon another, breaks the mold. And in his later work he has dispensed with walls altogether: *After the Fall* (1964) and the *Ride Down Mt. Morgan* are set inside a man's mind: the past conflates with the present and, in the case of *Mt. Morgan,* there is no consistent guideline to the reality of the action—the partition separating the exterior and interior life of the hero is permeable if not porous.

But why this playwright's reputation as a naturalist endures is an interesting question. It could have to do with the fact that when he writes a play the social context of his characters' lives is given full due. People live inseparable from their times. The capitalist ethos is visible in the slump of Willy Loman's shoulders. Gross crises of history, the Depression, the Holocaust, are not only reported by the characters but are mirrored in their personal calamities. In the late play *Broken Glass* (1994), the domestic tragedy of a Jewish accountant and his mysteriously afflicted wife in Brooklyn in 1938 is seen as a kind of transmuted *krystalnacht*. In *Mt. Morgan,* Lyman Felt, the self-involved lover of two women, is as contemporary as the gossip out of Washington. His bigamous heart is without a doubt a fin de siècle organ.

Another reason for Miller's misidentification as a naturalist is his unfailing ear for the speech of real life. He knows the way bank presidents speak, as well as lawyers, salesmen, wealthy Wasps, poor Jews, working-class Italians, old men, young men, brothers, fathers, women who are wives, women who are not wives.

Thus the theatergoer finds himself hearing the realistic dialogue of characters embroiled in a world historically familiar; that he is witnessing a severely aesthetic form of drama whose revelations can verge on allegory may be less apparent to him.

But is that bad? It may be a measure of his genius as an artificer that Arthur Miller is mistaken for a naturalist.

Unlike the scripts of many of his contemporaries, his bear reading. They read well, the music of the lines can be heard, and the elegance of their construction—in the logician's meaning of elegance as the exclusion of the inessential—can be appreciated. The theatergoer who has the chance to read published editions of the plays will make additional discoveries, chief among them that in the Millerian universe the drastic moral failings of human beings invariably play out as forms of self-deception. Nobody is simply posited as evil, as Iago, for example, is evil, or Edmund, the bastard son of Gloucester in *King Lear.* The birds come home to roost because evil has been done in the delusion of doing good. Eddie Carbone of *A View from the Bridge* cannot admit to himself his unnatural love for his niece. He thinks he is protecting her. And in *Broken Glass,* the accountant Phillip Gellburg must give himself a heart attack before he can acknowledge the destructiveness to himself and to his family of his Jewish self-hatred. These men are given to controlling not only themselves but the people around them. They rationalize their compulsion as love. And in the morally complex vision of this author it is, it is also and exactly love.

The hero of *Mt. Morgan,* Lyman Felt, in the aftermath of that punishing ride, undergoes something like a confessional review of his life's relationships. As does Quentin in *After the Fall,* he puts himself on trial. The defense arguments are made and made well, but if there is redemption for a Miller protagonist, it is in his self-judgment of moral insufficiency: the defense forever rests and, however ruefully, embraces the truth that has so long been resisted.

So that among the protagonists of these plays, there are those incapable of self-reflection who choose rather to destroy themselves . . . and those who undergo the crisis of self-revelation and find some means of stumbling on. What we as audience are left with in any event is a sense of moral consequence that brings us back to ourselves. We begin to appreciate the dimensions of human failing. But there are no easy answers. Those cast out from one's fortressed consciousness are fortressed as well. Lyman Felt says, "A man can be faithful to himself or to other people—but not to both." That is one tough line and it could not be uttered in a facile moralistic tale.

Like most authors, Arthur Miller has his obsessions, the ideas or archetypes he returns to again and again. He is preoccupied by the familial structures of father and son, brother and brother, husband and wife and second wife. And quite understandably he finds ways to return thematically to the Holocaust. There is a calculus in his overriding concern for individual moral failure: he proposes that the major social catastrophes, such as the Holocaust, are compounded of the prior cowardices, self-delusions, and rationalized cruelties of ordinary individual lives. Insofar as this suggests that we all live with a Nazi inside us—well, not everyone will agree. But no one can deny the courage of a writer who will say so. Nor deny his vision that we all connect in ways that we court disaster not to understand.

13.

Franz Kafka's *Amerika*

IN 1912, THE TWENTY-NINE-YEAR-OLD FRANZ KAFKA, a life-long resident of Prague whose occasional travels had taken him no farther than Paris, decided to write a novel set in America. We might wonder why, except that the United States had by then clearly emerged as a world power and a focal point for universal aspiration. To a German-speaking Czech Jewish writer gravely aware of living in a deadeningly historicized world, the idea of a New World would have a certain scintillation. This was to be Kafka's first novel, and though he'd never been to America, he seemed confident that he could compensate for his ignorance by diligent research. According to his biographer Ernst Pawel, Kafka read American travel books, attended lectures, collected printed materials, and spoke with returning emigrants, all for the purpose of writing a realistic novel authenticated with "up-to-date" American detail.

We will always revere genius, but we love it only when it doesn't know itself. In Kafka's *Amerika* the Statue of Liberty greets transoceanic arrivals with a raised sword. The port of New York presumably has no ship berths; when young Karl Rossmann, Kafka's immigrant hero, debarks from his liner he is rowed to shore. Staying at an uncle's well-appointed Manhattan apartment, Karl lies flat in a bathtub the size of a room and is sprayed from numerous shower heads. His uncle is a "Senator" who seems to have no role in government, the usage connoting a titled rank, such as Count or Baron. When Karl leaves the city he runs into a strike of metal workers picketing in a suburb that suggests Scarsdale. He is a guest in a suburban home in which servants, in full livery, walk about the drafty castle-like corridors with huge candelabra held in both hands. Karl travels deeper into the country along highways implanted with towers from which police direct the traffic. Tilled farm fields have tenements rising from them. A country town, presumably in upstate New York, has a subway system. A hotel is staffed by a hierarchy of uniformed professionals of the servant class, from imperial headwaiters down to overworked bellhops. When people on the street are stopped by the police, they must show their identity papers.

Kafka wrote two drafts before he abandoned the manuscript, unfinished, which suggests self-admitted failure—but in what sense? The work places *Popular Mechanics* notions of modernity in a Central European landscape. Had he failed his intention to write a realistic novel, or had he failed his vision?

The vast foreign literature of the obsession with America offers, as exemplary authors of the genre, Tocqueville and Dickens, who, like so many others, came across to see firsthand the biggest news story of their time and went back to record their impressions. But there is a subgenre of American studies that, derived from secondary sources, is visionary, factually unreliable, exploitative, and sometimes ludicrous. In this category we find works as notable as Bertolt Brecht's *Arturo Ui,* a play set in the meatpacking quarter of Chicago, or his *Mahagonny,* which sings lyrically of a full moon over the state of Alabama (both works written before Brecht ever arrived on these shores), but also the German-language potboilers of Karl May, who wrote scores of widely read novels of the American Wild West without having ventured out of Saxony.

It does not denigrate *Amerika* to locate it in this company. To find Franz Kafka in indiscriminate association with a major political dramatist, let alone a commercial hack, is to feel an almost messianic generosity in him. In the end, his innocent if not self-deluding researches, so screwily applied, portray America as a place no one has yet seen in a historical period that can't be identified. Incapable of realistic documentation, unlike his beloved Dickens, and only obliquely alluding to the stock of American myth, Kafka made his first novel from his own mind's mythic elements. And the research data that caught his eye were bent like light rays in a field of gravity.

This same brilliant force of mind effectively parodies, if it doesn't demolish, the narrative convention Kafka employs. *Amerika* is a picaresque. The hero, Karl Rossmann, sixteen years old, banished from his family's home for supposedly having sired a child by a housemaid, comes to the New World to make a new life. After a time in New York he leaves for the hinterland. He has adventures. He meets and travels with scoundrels. He gets into scrapes. He suffers injustice. We see him at the end heading west for a job in Oklahoma (what sort of job is another matter). To an American reader this is inescapably a road novel, and in its conclusive move westward satisfies the requirements of all our picaresque heroes, including Huck Finn. But if spaciousness, vista, light and air, and freedom are the circumstances of the genre, they are not much in evidence here.

Amerika subverts its convention by being a claustrophobic road novel. Karl Rossmann's recurring predicament is to be confined in small spaces. Before he even comes ashore in America he finds himself pressed into the bunk of the small steerage room belonging to the ship's stoker, where he has wandered by accident in the course of looking for his umbrella. The only way he can fit into the room is by lying down in the bunk; the stoker, a huge, much aggrieved man, pins him there, as much with his complaints about his job as with his bulk. Ashore, as a guest in the country home of a friend of his uncle, Karl spends the time trying politely to release himself from the clutches of the man's daughter, from the odd importunings of the man himself, who interviews him from a seated position, pressing Karl between his knees, and from the dark maze of corridors of the house itself. In subsequent chapters Karl will work twelve-hour shifts in an elevator and be sequestered in an attic with strangers, constrained in a porter's cubicle, imprisoned in a bedroom, and trapped on a balcony.

No matter where Karl's adventures take him, a certain social order prevails that negates his will and subjects him to the demands and desires of others. In the mythic land of freedom, his life is one of subjection, while all around him people have license to express their often terrible natures. He will find himself obligated to receive a variety of unwelcome attentions, including physical abuse. Often, the remarks addressed to him have a cryptic, ambiguously menacing quality. We might be tempted to read the book as a parable of the relationship of children and adults, Karl, after all, being a sixteen-year-old and younger than most of the people whose personalities he suffers. But we are reading Kafka: the parables we will get from him are not de-signed as sociological observation.

The title *Amerika* was chosen by Kafka's literary executor, Max Brod, who assembled the uncompleted manuscript and published it, as he did most of Kafka's work, after the writer's death. Kafka's working title was *The Man Who Disappeared (Der Verschollene)*. Men who are exiled disappear, of course, but they may also disappear from a loss of personality or moral integrity and by being metaphysical ephemera. What is the nature of Karl's disappearance? He is intelligent, quite adult, really, except perhaps for an incomplete awareness of female and possibly male expressions of sexual desire for him. On occasion he is actually capable of speaking up for himself, or of resisting what someone wants of him, or of questioning someone's behavior. But some-how the end result is always the same. Either his timing is not right or his spirit fails him. He tries to get out of a tight situation when, as a practical matter, he can't, and he doesn't try when he can. His experience as a young man on the road in a foreign country presupposes his sentimental education. But while he has learned English well enough, in pursuing his in-tention to make something of himself, he knows no more at the end, on his way to Oklahoma, than he did at the beginning, getting off the boat.

What is most confined and subject, in this fiction, is the hero's mind. It is not limited by intelligence, it is limited by the circumstances in which it finds itself. It is a mind contingent, a mind situated in the situation. Karl Rossmann, alone in a for-eign country, is totally engaged, moment by moment, in analyz-ing and evaluating his choices in the face of the expectations or demands of others. By giving patient and often exhaustive consideration to Karl's struggle, which is always his attempt to assimilate, Kafka proposes the paradox: that since Karl's mind is totally taken up or absorbed by the strange, inconsiderate, sometimes dangerous and always unpredictable America in which he finds himself, he is assimilated; at the same time, this constant and unending occupation of his mind ensures that he will be forever estranged.

Kafka loved the work of Heinrich von Kleist, the great early-nineteenth-century German writer whose chronicle fiction—written with a repertorial objectivity from an Olympian distance—had some influence on his own narrative strategy. Kafka applies the technique of the momentous Kleistian narrative to the minutiae of Karl Rossmann's discomforts. This may account for the sometimes sepulchral amusement of tone that preempts or modifies our own inclination to laugh. It may also contribute to what is uncanny in the tale, its oxymoronic aspect of elusive allegory, which is to say our feeling that there is such linear precision in the prose as to want to deny the mystery that it has for us.

At times Kafka would seem to define the spiritual quest as the struggle to meet one's obligations without too much loss of self-respect. As readers, we have the choice of interpreting him as an appalling satirist or as the prophet of an intolerable truth. As American readers, we have the additional problem of judging the likeness of our portrait. What we find unsettling is that Kafka came upon us first, *Amerika* being the earliest of his major metaphors of displacement, *The Trial, The Castle,* and *In the Penal Colony* coming later. The question must be asked if there is really no exemption for us from Kafka's prophecy, if he is not so totally Mitteleuropean in his flat characterizations of vile human nature, his depiction of the inevitable tyranny of all social structures, his mordant metaphysics of the emptiness of human striving. Why, for instance, can there not be consolation in the however imperfect American pursuit of a just social order under principles of the democratic Enlightenment? Even if men and women may only someday be released from the most dire problems of survival, they at least have the illusion of their own dignity, and some hope from their free pursuit of knowledge that the species can someday climb out of its epistemological hole—isn't that so? After all, how much of America is in *Amerika*?

Kafka gives us an old-fashioned political campaign rally toward the end of the book, a rally Karl observes from an apartment balcony where he is pressed between the bodies of his road companions, the scoundrels Delamarche and Robinson, and the fat lady, Brunelda, who has taken them in:

> Down below the main body of the procession had now come into sight behind the band. On the shoulders of a gigantic man sat a gentleman of whom nothing could be seen at this height save the faint gleam of a bald crown, over which he was holding a top-hat upraised in perpetual greeting. Round about him great wooden placards were being carried which, seen from the balcony, looked blankly white. . . . In the darkness, the whole breadth of the street, although only a trifling part of its length, was filled with the gentleman's supporters, who clapped their hands in rhythm and kept proclaiming in a chanting cadence what seemed to be the gentleman's . . . short but incomprehensible name. Single supporters . . . were

carrying motor-car lamps of enormous power, which they slowly shone up and down the houses on both sides of the street. . . . On the balconies where supporters of the candidate were packed, the people joined in chanting his name, stretching their hands far over the railings and clapping with machine-like regularity. On the opposition balconies . . . a howl of retaliation arose. . . . All the enemies of the . . . candidate united in a general cat-calling. . . . Here and there unrecognisable objects were being flung by particularly heated partisans . . . into the street, where they provoked yells of rage.

Trapped as Karl may be on that odd, incongruous balcony, one of a townful apparently, there is no saving alternative for him in the numbers below. Kafka would seem to equate democracy with mob life. So we are given intimation of the madness, if not the barbarism, of all culture. We may argue that this is an American political rally seen, so to speak, from a European balcony. But perhaps this is the occasion in our reading when we have to grant Kafka's genius the moral right to bend his research, disdain all thought of verisimilitude, and depict our landscape in the imagery of his own Central Europe. Can there be such a thing as a New World after all? The America of *Amerika* is a European transplant, yes, just as it might be said by the Dutch and Spanish and English and French that America is, in historical fact, a transplant. And if the police did not ask people on the street for their identity papers in 1913, can we say they won't be more likely to do so in 2013?

But no consideration of the truth of Kafka's rendering is possible without special attention to the book's gloriously insane last chapter entitled by Max Brod "The Nature Theatre of Oklahoma." The Nature Theatre has set up a recruitment center in the open space of a racetrack. "Everyone is welcome!" Karl reads on a billboard. "If you want to be an artist, join our company! Today only and never again! If you miss your chance now you miss it forever!"

Never revealed is how Karl has escaped his overbearing companions Delamarche and Robinson—it is one of the problems of plot Kafka left unsolved. At the racetrack entrance is a long platform on which hundreds of young women stand atop pedestals "dressed as angels in white robes with great wings on their shoulders [and] blowing on long trumpets that glittered like gold." Karl is inspired to borrow a trumpet for a moment and play along with them. He then enters the track itself, where Nature Theatre employment bureaus have been set up in the bookmakers' booths. After a series of interviews, in which he is referred by virtue of his lack of profession and education to more and more modest categories of employment, he arrives at the last booth, where one's name is the only credential one need present for employment. It comes as almost a physical shock to the reader when Karl gives his name: "Negro," he says. This is the moment when our confident American exceptionalism may be shaken, the moment when we find that dark glittering-eyed, sad-smiling face of Franz Kafka reading with us, right over our shoulder, his story after all, telling of a kind of slavery.

Karl Rossmann is hired as an actor, and after he partakes of a big picnic for the new employees, he boards a train with the others and sets out to Oklahoma with some hope for his future and trust in the enterprise he has joined. The train journey begins, but before it comes to its destination the narrative breaks off, and we have had as much Kafka in America as we are going to get.

Our questions multiply. Why a racetrack? Why Oklahoma? The luminous surrealism of the chapter is its own justification— it is as right as Lewis Carroll. But we may refer finally to Kafka's misperceived, or brilliantly metaphorized, research from secondary sources, and imagine ourselves in arrogance as witnesses to the epiphanic moment when this genius read of the various Homestead Acts of the nineteenth century by which, for example, any American was entitled to a grant of 160 acres of the Oklahoma Territory if he was willing to get on his horse and race thousands of others just like him across the scrublands. The dream conflation of historical elements here into a heavenly intervention complete with trumpets, as if the buffeting Kafka's young hero has taken until now has been no more than a test of character, probably accounts for the critical consensus that this is Kafka's most optimistic work, Kafka Lite, as it were, a judgment that seems to have been the author's as well. I cannot share it. More likely, it is Kafka the first novelist just beginning to discover what he can and can't do. All first novels are necessarily exercises in literary self-definition. *Amerika* is not optimistic, it is the work of a writer not fully arrived: the realm of what we call the Kafkaesque is still some kilometers away, or down.

We are not too far wrong to see in Karl Rossmann the explorer who maps the internal territory for the later Kafka hero Joseph K. of *The Trial*. It is a natural segue, after all, from the youth who lives to placate . . . to the adult with the inescapable sense of guilt. In fact, we could propose Kafka as an artist in life-long search of the most accommodating conceit for his vision.

Karl is the earliest of his eponymous heroes, all of them, through all the work, essentially one tormented soul whose hallucinatory landscape keeps changing.

The open-air Nature Theatre chapter was the last writing Kafka did on *Amerika*. At the point he broke the book's claustrophobic hold, at the moment he granted his road hero light and open space and fresh air, he couldn't continue. Why? We can speculate that by this time the book had taught him what he needed to know. More specifically, that the American experience, and the specifics of its slave-ridden history, had an innate metaphorical self-sufficiency, that it was irreducible, and therefore, finally, a different nightmare from his own. Or perhaps that American geography was too problematical—that he'd held his book together as long as he'd ignored the true scale of the American continent—and that the minute he tried to fold our vast openness into his conceit he was finished.

Kafka would always have difficulty with the longer form of the novel. His purely linear narratives, unembellished and single-minded, were easily tempted into the stillness of iconography. (His stylistic master Heinrich von Kleist never ventured a length longer than the novella.) Not only *Amerika* but *The Trial* and *The Castle* would remain unfinished. But what *Amerika* taught him was crucial: that the story he had to tell took place in a territory darker and more hermetic than the American West, that it would be fully told before Karl Rossmann could even board a ship to go to America, and that, exile only reiterating the original universal banishment from Heaven, a man might disappear down the stark, unmediated horrors of his own consciousness without ever leaving the house in which he was born.

14.

W. G. Sebald

ONCE UPON A TIME, when the only authors were God and his prophets, stories were presumed to be true simply by the fact of being told. No more. In a modern world deprived by rationalism and science of a divinely conceived universe, all authors are recognized as mortal. Their stories are not automatically believed to be true. This creates a problem that writers writing in the name of God never had. And so, since the appearance of the earliest novels, authors have had to reclaim the authority of their art by ruse.

Cervantes tells us in Part 1 of *Don Quixote* that he found the manuscript of the don's adventures in a marketplace in Toledo—as written by an Arab historian. Daniel Defoe writes in his introduction to *Robinson Crusoe* that he has functioned only as its editor. Cervantes and Defoe claim authority for their stories—as history, as biography, as truth—by denying their own authorship. In recent times, the techniques by which fiction writers claim legitimacy are more various and more subtle: simulations of unmediated consciousness, as in James Joyce or Virginia Woolf, or the stratagem of the self-doubting narrative, as in various works of postmodernism.

The late W. G. Sebald's recourse—a return to the implicit denial of imaginative authorship—has been so masterfully conceived (his fictions are mélanges of travel writing, memoir, essay, photographs, diaries, and spoken reminiscence by subjects sought out and found in the midst of meticulously described settings) that his works, such as *The Emigrants,* have puzzled some critics and are seen as some new undefined thing—perhaps not fiction at all. Yet he is only following the road taken by the itinerant don, if some dark European centuries later.

Sebald himself said in an interview with Arthur Lubow, "There is so often about the standard novel something terribly contrived. . . . The business of having to have bits of dialogues move the plot along, that's fine for an eighteenth- or nineteenth-century novel, but that becomes in our day a bit trying, where you always see the wheels of the novel grinding and going on." *But that becomes in our day a bit trying?* This is not the remark of a journalist or a scholar for whom there is no question of fiction's reduced authority. There is too much complaint in it to be anything other than the sentiment of a practitioner, too much of a sense of the burdened storyteller who has given himself the desperate task of trying to make it new.

The Emigrants is a work of fiction, a composition of expropriated genres recognized to have authority in a factually driven world.

What Sebald has kept of the nineteenth-century novel is its love of exposition, its descriptive patience, and the confident relaxation of the narrative bond—the loss of tension—that is so inevitable in most of the great six-hundred- and eight-hundred-page nineteenth-century tomes. He has cultivated that to the point of perversity: his stories have no plot, no obvious suspense; they are without exchanges of dialogue, or expressed conflicts, and receive no momentum from the linear presentation of time.

Each of the four stories that make up *The Emigrants* gives us the life and past of a Jewish or part-Jewish survivor of the European Holocaust of the 1930s and '40s. But there are none of the general statements that would seem necessary in a work of serious historical dimension: I think the word *Nazi* appears just once in the book. Those who don't survive—the relatives, the mothers and fathers, the lovers—simply disappear from the narrative. The Holocaust is indicated by the quiet dissolution of family life. And so we recognize another traditional storytelling device—the withholding of information—in this case any detailed account of the monumental European disaster that has left the emigrants, who have presumably escaped with their lives, as living dead.

All four sections of *The Emigrants* are the narrative of a curious and reflective voice of judicious intelligence—a nameless emigrant himself whose own itinerancy is unexplained and so seems to carry the heritage of displacement given him by the survivors he ferrets out, survivors from an older generation than his own. And since he is a person, a speaking voice, and some of what has to be divulged of these other lives he cannot possibly have witnessed himself, the same narrative voice is regularly transferred to others, in their reminiscences, their diaries, so that we are always in the first person, and in the consistent tone of the same sensibility, but with the certainty of truth of the oral history. Sebald of course knew the work of Joseph Conrad, who is a master of this nest-of-boxes technique.

But that is just one of the writerly habits that characterize Sebald's fiction. The memories that are evoked are so specific and detailed and thickly textured that they are humanly impossible: they are memories beyond the capacity of actual nonliterary memory. Time and time again we are given reminiscences of the loveliness of ordinary living before the sweep of the scythe: life that is exquisitely modest, preciously unassuming, family oriented, charmingly eccentric, and above all rooted, deeply rooted, in the presumption of European civilization, and so, doomed to be betrayed.

Much discussion of Sebald revolves around the black-and-white photographs that appear throughout his work. Are they supposed to be taken as illustrations of what the text describes, or do they complement the text less exactly, more mysteriously? Or both. To me, however, and perhaps to other working writers who find themselves haunted by photographs of those who have gone before, they are catalysts for his creative thinking—they are like the fermenting apples in Balzac's desk drawer; they are Proust's madeleine—and, as perhaps the most honest of writers, Sebald has left them in the book they have helped create. I recognize in his use of such pictures—pictures from his own background, but more often found photos of people he has never known—that basic impulse of the artist to put things together that have never before been put together.

Running like leitmotifs through these stories are ritually meticulous accounts of what one sees when one moves from place to place, by air, by water, by foot, and almost obsessive descriptions of places come to, and of their inevitable ruin—a garden gone to seed; a city, Manchester, gone to industrial decay—as equivalents of the lives ruined and gone to seed of the people he finds there. And despite his theme, he is not beyond playfulness: the reader will find in all four pieces the cameo role of a man who nets butterflies—in the form in one instance of a photo of Vladimir Nabokov, whose habit of writing down precisely his quotidian experiences on filing cards may have taught Sebald the way to assemble his own exacting descriptions—and who seems meant to symbolize some glorious passion of innocence.

Finally, it is the habit of several of his characters to escape from their anxiety or dread by seeking out the high mountains, in the Alps, the Jura, where invariably they reflect on the beauty of the deceptively peaceful world below that will soon be unavailable to them—if it ever was.

In the aftermath of Sebald's shocking death in 2001 in an automobile accident, it may seem inappropriate to speak of his writing strategies, to indicate in part how the stories in *The Emigrants* work and how they participate in literary tradition. But I would offer these observations as an homage. We mourn Sebald as a supremely gifted colleague of our generation partly from the sense of recognition we have for what he has made with the materials we have all been given.

And of course, finally, something comes off the pages that defies analysis. From the modulations of his sentences and the paradoxes built into them, we infer a culture of rarefied sensibility that seems to be the florescence of a dying civilization. As if there could not be such exquisite humanity as he describes except at the cessation of social life. The continent traveled by these emigrants seems used up—used up by all the living that has been done on it, all the armies that have trod upon it, all the blood that has poured into it.

W. G. Sebald is an elegist. Here on this continent we have to hope that he is not a prophet.

15.

Einstein
Seeing the Unseen

WHEN I WAS A STUDENT at the Bronx High School of Science in New York City, our principal, Dr. Morris Meister, had an image for scientific endeavor and the enlightenment it brings: "Think of science as a powerful searchlight continuously widening its beam and bringing more of the universe into the light," he said. "But as the beam of light expands, so does the circumference of darkness."

That image would certainly have appealed to Albert Einstein, whose lifelong effort to find the few laws that would explain all physical phenomena ran into immense difficulties as the revolutionary light of his theory of relativity discerned a widening darkness.

Of course, to a public celebrating its own mystification, that hardly mattered. The incomprehensibility of his space-time physics, and the fulfillment of an early prophecy of the theory of relativity when Sir Arthur Eddington's experiments confirmed the bending of starlight as it passed by the sun, was enough for Einstein to be exalted as the iconic genius of the twentieth century.

This was a role he could never seriously accept; he would come to enjoy its perks and use it as he grew older on behalf of his various political and social causes, but his fame was an irrelevancy at best and did not accord with the reality of a life lived most of the time in a state of intellectual perplexity. To be a genius to someone else was not to be a genius to oneself. Acts of mind always come without a rating.

Einstein would say by way of calming his worldwide admirers, "In science . . . the work of the individual is so bound up with that of his scientific predecessors and contemporaries that it appears almost as an impersonal product of his generation."

Could this statement have been something more than an expression of modesty on his part?

Einstein came of age in a culture that was in hot pursuit of physical laws. In Europe some of his scientific elders—Albert Michelson and Edward Morley, Hermann Helmholtz, Heinrich Hertz, and Ernst Mach, to name a few—determined that electromagnetic waves move through space at the speed of light; their work called into question the concepts of absolute motion and absolute rest, everything in the universe moving only in relation to something else. So the science leading up to Einstein's breakthrough was in a sense premonitory—it gave him the tools with which to think.

If we look outside the scientific enterprise of his time to the culture in general, we discover that this same turn-of-the-century period in which Einstein conceived his theory of relativity put him in the national German-speaking Jewish company of such contemporaries as Sigmund Freud, Franz Kafka, the revolutionary atonalist composer Arnold Schoenberg, the critic Walter Benjamin, the great anthropologist Franz Boas, and the philosopher of symbolic forms Ernst Cassirer. They joined the still-living precedent generation of Friedrich Nietzsche, who had proclaimed that God is dead, and Gustav Mahler, whose freewheeling First Symphony was written while Einstein was still a child. Mahler's First, a big kitchen sink of a symphony, with its openness to idea, its structural relaxations, its excesses of voice and extravagance of mood, all coming after the unified and majestic sonorities of Brahms, for example, was in effect a kind of news broadcast: "This just in: the nineteenth-century world is coming apart."

Frederic V. Grunfeld's book *Prophets Without Honor* is the definitive account of this cultural florescence of German-speaking Jews. A multibiographical study of some of the artists and intellectuals of the period, it finds as their common characteristic not only an intense work ethic but also a passion that would drive them to take on the deepest and most intransigent questions. As Freud would plumb the unconscious in his effort to "understand the origin and nature of human behavior," so Einstein would set off on his lifelong quest for a unified field theory that would encompass all physical phenomena.

Of course, outside Germany some world-shattering things were going on as well: in Paris, Braque's and Picasso's cubist paintings and Stravinsky's *The Rite of Spring*, which brought on a riot at its premiere; in Bologna, Marconi's experiments with radio waves; at Kitty Hawk, the Wright brothers' first flight. So Einstein came of age at a moment not only in German culture but in world history—those early years of the twentieth century—that if I were a transcendentalist I might consider as manifesting the activity of some sort of stirred-up world oversoul.

The English poet and essayist Matthew Arnold speaks about such historic moments of creative arousal in literature in his 1865 essay "The Function of Criticism at the Present Time." "The grand work of literary genius," says Arnold, "is a work of synthesis and exposition . . . its gift lies in the faculty of being happily inspired by a certain intellectual and spiritual atmosphere, by a certain order of ideas, when it finds itself in them; of dealing divinely with these ideas. . . . But it must have the atmosphere, it must find itself amidst the order of ideas, in order to work freely; and these it is not so easy to command. This is why great creative epochs in literature are so rare; this is why there is so much that is unsatisfactory in the productions of many men of real genius; because for the creation of a masterwork of literature two powers must concur, the power of the man and the power of the moment, and the man is not enough without the moment."

Arnold's thesis puts me in mind of the debate among historians of science as to whether science at its most glorious (for example, the work of Copernicus, Galileo, Darwin, or Einstein) is a revolution or whether it emerges incrementally as evolution. Perhaps it is both evolutionary and revolutionary. Perhaps there *is* an evolving communal intellect, and its role is periodically to be stunned and possibly outraged by the revolutionary ideas that it had not realized it was itself fomenting.

Thus, to speak of the power of the moment does not gainsay the power of the man. Opinions vary as to when, if ever, the theory of relativity might have been articulated if Einstein had not lived. Some scholars have said it would have taken generations. The eminent English astrophysicist Sir Martin Rees believes that it would have been conceived by now, but not by just one theorist working alone.

So what are we to make of Einstein's own reference to the communal context of creativity, whereby the scientific work of an individual "appears almost as an impersonal product of his generation"? As always, he was being totally honest. Yet we must ask to whom the work appears as an impersonal product— certainly not to the world that applauds it and names its producer a genius. Rather it appears impersonal to the producer himself, the revelation of such work coming to his mind always as a deliverance, at a moment in his thought when his personality, his psyche, is released from itself in the transcendent freedom of a revelation.

The creative act doesn't fulfill the ego but rather changes its nature. You are less than the person you usually are.

Einstein's theory of relativity was an arduous work of self-expression no less than that of a great writer or painter. It was not accomplished without enormous mental struggle. It was created not merely from an intellectual capacity but also from an internal demand of his character that must have defined itself in his nightmares as Atlas holding up the sky with his shoulders. It was a matter of urgency to figure things out lest the universe be so irrational that it would come down around his and everyone else's head. The term *obsession* is woefully insufficient to describe a mind so cosmologically burdened.

We have to assume also that there was the occasion of lightning clarity when that formula $E = mc^2$ wrote itself in his brain, the moment of creative crisis, the eureka moment. And here a writer can only scrub about in his own field to find a writer's equivalent moment, as described by a giant of his profession, Henry James.

In his essay "The Art of Fiction," James speaks of the "immense sensibility . . . that takes to itself the faintest hints of life . . . and converts the very pulses of the air into revelations." He celebrates the novelist's intuitive faculty "to guess the unseen from the seen," but the word *guess* may be inadequate, for it is a power, I think, generated by the very discipline to which the writer is committed. The discipline itself is empowering, so that a sentence spun from the imagination confers on the writer a degree of perception or acuity or heightened awareness that a sentence composed with the strictest attention to fact does not.

Every author from the writers of the ancient sacred texts to James himself has relied on that empowering paradox. It involves the working of our linguistic minds on the world of things-in-themselves. We ascribe meaning to the unmeant, and the sentences form with such synaptic speed that the act of writing, when it is going well, seems no more than the dutiful secretarial response to a silent dictation.

This feeling, I suggest, may be the same as the scientist's in his eureka moment, when what he has discovered by seeing past the seen to the unseen has the character of appearing as "an impersonal product of his generation."

And there must be something common to the creative act, whatever its discipline, in James's assertion that from one evocative fragment of conversation overheard by the writer an entire novel can be written, that from the slightest bit of material a whole novelistic world is created. We may represent this as the Little Bang of the writer's or scientist's inspiration, thinking analogously of the Big Bang, that prime-moving happenstance when the universe blew out into its dimensions, exploding in one silent flash into the volume and chronology of space-time.

If the analogy seems grandiose, I remind myself that the writers of the ancient texts, the sacred texts of our religions, attributed the Little Bang of their own written cosmologies not to the impersonal product of their generation but to God. The God of the universe was the author of what they wrote, so awed were they by the mystery of their own creative process.

But whether the creative mind feels it is dutifully transcribing a silent dictation, or that its work appears almost as an impersonal product of a generation, or that it is serving as a medium for the voice of God, what is always involved is a release from personality, liberation, an unshackling from the self.

That self was wildly manifest in Einstein's youth, when he seems to have renounced both his German citizenship and his Jewish faith; it was manifest in his adulthood during the course of two difficult marriages and an affinity for extramarital wandering. His biographers tell us how, in his student days as an assimilated Jewish boy in a German gymnasium, one of his teachers held up a rusty nail and, looking directly at Albert, said such spikes were driven through Christ's hands and feet. That brought home to the boy the social isolation he was born to, a position he came to relish because looking in from the outside, he saw clearly the pretensions and lies and dogmas upon which the society fed. He would come to distrust every form of authority. He was from the beginning, as he himself said, "a free spirit."

It was in childhood that Einstein's difference as a quiet, unflinchingly observant Jewish kid allowed him to hone the skep-

ticism that as an adult he applied to intellectual postulates that
had been in place for centuries. His society's resentment grew as
Einstein's mind grew, exponentially. By the 1930s, a winner of
the Nobel Prize, he was at the top of Hitler's enemy list. He was
designated for assassination, and even when he was out of the
country, in Belgium, authorities insisted that he have body-
guards. Einstein's biographers agree that he was always philosophical, always calm in the face of personal danger. As his fame
grew, he had necessarily to apply his mind to social, political,
and religious issues. He brought to these nonscientific issues the
same clarity of thinking that was evident in the only definitions
of time and space that he could allow himself: time, "something
you measure with a clock," and space, "something you measure
with a ruler." God he called *Das Alte,* or "the Old One," iden-
tifying the only attribute of God he could be sure of—old in
nominal existence solely. He applied that same beautiful and
scrupulously pragmatic clarity of thought to the famous ethical
conundrum most forcefully postulated by Immanuel Kant: How
can there be an ethical system without an ultimate authority,
without the categorical imperative of an *ought*—in short, without God?

Here is how Einstein cut through that problem: "Ethical axioms are found and tested not very differently from the axioms
of science. Truth is what stands the test of experience," he said.
"For pure logic, all axioms are arbitrary, including the axioms of
ethics. But they are by no means arbitrary from a psychological
and genetic point of view. They are derived from our inborn
tendencies to avoid pain and annihilation, and from the accu-
mulated emotional reaction of individuals to the behavior of
their neighbors. It is the privilege of man's moral genius . . . to

advance ethical axioms which are so comprehensive and so well founded that men will accept them as grounded in the vast mass of their individual emotional experiences."

There is one more point to be made in the futile project of trying to plumb the creative mind of this genius: throughout his life he found excuses, almost apologies, for his prodigious accomplishment. "Sometimes I ask myself," he once said, "how it came about that I happened to be the one to discover the theory of relativity. The reason is, I think, that the normal adult never stops to think about space and time. Whatever thinking he may do about these things he will already have done as a small child. I, on the other hand, was so slow to develop that I only began thinking about space and time when I was already grown up. Naturally, I then went more deeply into the problem than an ordinary child."

Einstein had a sense of humor; a sly diffidence was one of his stocks-in-trade when dealing with the press, and this was a sweetly funny thing to say—except that in this case I think he was quite serious. For hidden in this remark is an acceptance of himself as an eternal child. This prodigy of thought was eternally a child prodigy. And if that would seem to diminish the man, remember that it was a child who cried out that the emperor had no clothes. All his life Einstein would point to this or that ruling thought and reveal its nakedness, until finally it was the prevailing universe that had no clothes.

Dare we think that a mind of this immensity—independent, self-directed with such a penetrating clarity of thought, and driven with a rampant curiosity—must have had, too, a protective naïveté about the nature of itself? There was a confidence in reality that must have protected him from the philosophical despair of Ludwig Wittgenstein, another genius born to the power of the moment, just ten years after Einstein, and the most influential European philosopher of his generation.

Wittgenstein revolutionized philosophy by dismissing everyone from Plato to Hegel as purveyors of metaphysical nonsense. All philosophy could do was to logically understand thought. He was a philosopher of language who used linguistic analysis to distinguish those propositions that were meaningful from those that had no justifiable connection to the existing world. "The meaning is the use," he said. Wittgenstein's philosophy, a technique more than a teaching, was almost directly attributable to the appropriation by science of the great cosmological questions that had traditionally been the province of philosophy. Certainly Einstein's discoveries were the salients of this scientific encroachment. Yet Wittgenstein believed that science, even at its most successful, by its nature could go only so far. He articulated the most desolate intellectual pronouncement of the twentieth century: "If all possible scientific questions are answered," said Wittgenstein, "our problem is still not touched at all."

What did he mean? He meant that even if Einstein, or we, find the final few laws to account for all phenomena, the unfathomable is still there. He meant that all science hits a wall.

Wittgenstein's is the steely gaze of the inconsolable and ultimately irretrievable spirit directed into the abyss of its own consciousness. His is the philosophical despair of a mind in the appalled contemplation of itself. Such a despair was not in the nature of Einstein's beautifully childlike contemplations.

Einstein was directed outward, his face pressed into the sky. The universe had always been there, as it was, regardless of how it was conceived by humanity, and so the great enterprise was to understand it as it was in the true laws by which it operated. It was a matter for wonder and mental industry. The crackling vastness of black holes and monumental conflagrations, the ineffable something rather than nothing, such an indifference to life as to make us think that if God is involved in its creation he is so fearsome as to be beyond any human entreaty for our solace or comfort or the redemption that would come of our being brought into his secret—this consideration did not seem to be part of Einstein's cosmology.

Einstein's life spanned the terrors of the twentieth century—two world wars, the worldwide Great Depression, fascism, communism, the Holocaust, the threat of nuclear war—and he was never less than steadfast and rational in his attention to the history of his time. He lived as he thought, in the thrill of the engagement. He was a scientist, a secular humanist, a democratic socialist, a Zionist, a pacifist, an antinuclear activist, and never, so far as I know, did he succumb to a despair of human life. So finally, even if in his Einsteinian pragmatism God could only be accurately described as the Old One, surely there was a faith in that image, perhaps an agnostic's faith, that made it presumptuous for any human being to come to any conclusion about the goodness or incomprehensible amorality of God's universe or the souls it contained until we at least learned the laws that governed it.

For Albert Einstein a unified field theory needn't be the end. It can just as well be the beginning.

16.

The Bomb

In 1943, with the war against Japan intensifying in the Pacific, Dr. L. F. Fisser of the National Defense Research Committee designed a tiny incendiary bomb for the use of the U.S. Army Air Forces. The two-ounce bomb was to be dropped on Japan affixed to free-tailed bats (*Tadarida brasiliensis*), of which there happened to be an ample supply in Carlsbad Caverns, New Mexico. The bat bombs were to be chilled to hibernating temperature in ice-cube trays, packed 180 to a box, and sprung free at a thousand feet above the ground, where they would thaw and, in great hunger, swoop down on the wood and paper homes of Tokyo.

Something may be insane, but it is crackpot only when it doesn't work. Another plan to bring the total warfare concept to the Japanese capital was conceived by General Curtis LeMay. Using B-29 bombers as they had not been used before, he sent waves of them in low over Tokyo at night armed with one-hundred-pound oil-gel bombs and six-pound gelled-gasoline bombs. What came to be known as "the Great Tokyo Air Raid" burned out sixteen square miles of the city, leaving 100,000 people dead, a million wounded, and a million homeless. Only the powers of the mobilized human imagination—powers that verge on magic—could transform a blind shrieking bat with a little bomb clipped to its skin into a B-29.

The Japanese government, at the time xenophobic and racist, its people self-persuaded of their subjection to a living God, had its own considerable powers of military imagination. The military thought not of bats to fight their war, but they did have an ample supply of young men who could be turned into bombs—human bombs, human torpedoes, human mines—to fly, to dive, to swim, perchance to explode, against enemy armament. This was glory. This was a culture of contempt for individual life. In battle, troops were ordered to commit suicide rather than surrender. It is no wonder, with such twisted regard for their own, that Japanese commanders were uninhibitedly brutal to their prisoners of war and to their subject peoples in China, Korea, Burma. They worked over 100,000 of them to death building their Thailand-Burma railway.

But the ways of death in war are innumerable. The ethics of warfare are reconfigured to its changing technology. By 1945 there was no longer a viable distinction between combatants and noncombatants. Perhaps 51 million human beings were killed in the worldwide war that raged from 1939 to 1945. Bombed, firebombed, strafed, mined, suffocated, gassed, incinerated, frozen, mutilated, starved, beheaded, hanged, buried alive, and dissolved in a luminous flash. Certainly more than half of them died as civilians.

Twenty years before, another great war in Europe had killed its generation of young men, the fieldpieces drawn by horses, the ordnance in dinky trucks, though all of it sufficient unto the day, with Sten guns halving men on the dotted line, and mustard gas cauterizing their lungs, and some of those Big Berthas heaving three-hundred-pound shells in seventy-five-mile trajectories. But the technology was not yet developed for carpet-bombing cities behind the lines. There were still lines. Civilians could still be refugees clogging the roads with their carts of bedding, their hope chests, their children, while the troops pushed through them toward the front.

That was the war before the war. The twenty years or so between the war before the war, and the war after the war before the war, were hardly riven by peace. The new fascist military states field-tested their machines, dive-bombing Ethiopians who carried spears and strafing peasants on horseback in Spain. The concentration camp and the gulag were invented, genocide was the subject of secret planning sessions, and Hitler was using radio for purposes of mass hypnosis.

And so we come to the perverse and bitter fate of the international community of theoretical physicists who, swept up by the barbarities of the time, were driven out of Europe or inward to despair, and scattered among the nations that would once more war with one another. Their collegial exchanges of information were suspended. Their abstract considerations of the nature of the universe were suddenly and desperately practical. It became all too clear that the beauty of their calculations had hidden from them the terms of the truly Faustian contract they had somehow scratched their names to.

"Dear Sir," wrote Albert Einstein in a letter to President Franklin Roosevelt on August 2, 1939,

> Some recent work . . . leads me to expect that the element
> uranium may be turned into a new and important source of
> energy. . . . [I]t may become possible to set up nuclear chain

reactions. . . . Extremely powerful bombs of a new type may thus be constructed. . . . I understand that Germany has actually stopped the sale of uranium. . . . That she should have taken such early action might perhaps be understood on the ground that the son of the German Undersecretary of State, von Weizsäcker, is attached to the Kaiser Wilhelm Institute of Berlin, where some of the American work on uranium is now being repeated.

America made the A-bomb out of fear of the A-bomb. Its components were either uranium isotopes or plutonium, high-explosive lenses, bullets, tubes, steel frames, inner shells, outer casings, fins, neutrons, protons, radiant poisons, and a dread of the malignant war-machined sociopathy of Adolf Hitler. Industrializing our fear, we were soon effecting controlled chain reactions under the fieldhouse stands at the University of Chicago. Another year or two and we were thermally diffusing or extracting plutonium in Hanford, Washington, and Oak Ridge, Tennessee. We ran critical experiments at Columbia and Berkeley, and brought everything together for design and engineering at the secret community of brains in Los Alamos.

By 1944 the atom bomb was the employer of 129,000 people.

At the heart of it all, living in isolation at Los Alamos, the scientists and mathematicians and engineers enlisted for the enterprise worked long and hard hours on a two-track program, crafting one bomb that would have an internal firing mechanism to explode it, and devising a second that would implode. While they solved one design problem after another, the scintillations of their intellectual breakthroughs and discoveries were not always connected emotionally to the grim purposes behind them.

But of course they could never forget, and the work was not even finished before they began to say among themselves that the bomb must never be used. The energetic, chain-smoking Szilard, a Hungarian, began to circulate petitions. "Now I am become Death, the destroyer of worlds," said the presiding physicist and scholar of the Bhagavad Gita, Oppenheimer, when the Trinity test at White Sands went off with blinding magnitude like a born sun over the desert. Kistiakowsky called it the "nearest thing to Doomsday." Bethe, Peierls, Ulam, Rabi, all of them with such terrible sickening misgivings. And young Feynman, sitting over a beer, depressed, close to tears thinking of the number of people walking around at that moment who didn't know they were dead.

> . . . a ring of skull-
> bone fused to the inside of a helmet; a pair of eyeglasses
> taken off the eyes of a witness, without glass,
> which vanished, when a white flash sparkled.

is the way the poet Galway Kinnell puts it.

What is the mythic reference for such an event? Shiva? Prometheus? The Tree of Knowledge? None is sufficient. Participating cross-mythically in cultures that encompass the globe, the nuclear explosion must itself become a primary myth in the postnuclear world to come. It will become a scriptural text. At this time, with newly resurgent nations racing to acquire their own nuclear armories some sixty years after the dropping of the

bomb on Hiroshima and the second bomb over Nagasaki, and
the world war they concluded, and the Cold War thermonuclear Superbomb they generated, we see the lines beginning to
be drawn, the lineaments of conflicting accounts, as when in the
years of early Christianity the struggle began to turn history
into gospel.

As this age goes on, if we have the time, we will choose according to the society we conceive for ourselves the scientists,
politicians, generals, and spies whom we want for our story. It
will have Hiroshima and Nagasaki in it, of course; it will have
the Berlin wall, Korea, and the Cuban Missile Crisis. It will have
Harry S. Truman. He came into the presidency with the death
of Roosevelt in April 1945. The United States dropped its
bombs in August, just four months later. We will argue among
ourselves whether Truman made the crucial decisions or simply
let the years of war planning and military momentum work out
to their logical conclusion. We will argue about his need to
come out from under the shadow of a predecessor of whose
greatness there was no question in his mind. We will have to
compute the most likely number of lives of American soldiers
he saved by avoiding an invasion of the Japanese homeland. We
will have to decide how much the desire to cow the Russians
figured in his decision. We will eventually determine whether
the bomb had to be dropped at all, and if there was the need for
an invasion, given the wreckage of the Japanese war machine
and the signals sent by Japan that it was receptive to negotiating
a surrender. And if we decide the Hiroshima bomb had to be
dropped, we will need to know why the Nagasaki bomb had to
be dropped as well.

Examining the beginnings of the Cold War, we will have to

consider the character of Secretary of State James Byrnes, a South Carolinian and Truman appointee who insisted on making the bomb our postwar foreign policy and dismissed with fierce Southern contempt the international nuclear arms control advocates David Lilienthal and Dean Acheson. We will have to try to remember David Lilienthal and Dean Acheson.

If the atom bomb was fathered by Hitler, the hydrogen bomb belongs in part to Stalin—only in part because the arms race was as much a creation of our Cold War containment foreign policy as it was a result of Soviet actions. At one point soon after the end of World War II, we were flaunting our atomic stockpile when in fact we had no assembled bombs and the work at Los Alamos had ground to a halt; and the Russians on their end were making ominous warlike references to their immense land armies when in fact they were an exhausted people with 20 million dead, a ruined economy, and an infrastructure largely unrepaired from the German invasion.

Sitting on the other side of the world in Soviet Russia were the enemy's scientists, who relied on espionage reports to guide their research. Russian espionage was a major industry. During the early days of Lend-Lease they flew planefuls of technical information from Montana to Siberia—information from every conceivable field, including atomic research. Oppenheimer's counterpart was a Russian physicist named Igor Kurchatov, who read the espionage dispatches with the acuity of a capitalist reading stock quotations. The Soviet counterpart to General Leslie Groves, the director of the Manhattan Project, was the infamous Lavrenti Beria, Stalin's executioner and the head of the secret police, a fact of which the assembled physicists in their privileged dachas were only too aware. Their installation at Chelyabinsk was staffed with slave labor; their nuclear tests followed at regular lengths our tests at Bikini and Eniwetok. "Did it look like the American one?" Beria demanded to know once after a Russian blast.

The spies of the Cold War were an assortment of idiosyncratic emissaries between the two cultures, a strange, furtive lot of usually young idealists, not terribly smart amateurs here, like Julius Rosenberg, Harry Gold, and David Greenglass . . . and shrewder professionals in England, like Kim Philby and Donald Maclean and Guy Burgess. But the one who will most likely have a place in the postnuclear text appears now to be Klaus Fuchs, the young German Communist who was a superb scientist, a physicist of such repute that he worked in the inner circles both at Harwell in England and Los Alamos, from where he methodically leaked not only his own contributions but those of everyone else to his Soviet handlers. Vividly antifascist, he was personally drab, a joyless, unnaturally quiet fellow who contained in himself not only the scientist's torment of intellectual joy mixed with moral horror but the Soviet spy's anxiety of living dangerously in the West.

Richard Rhodes, in his exacting and compendious history of the hydrogen bomb enterprise, *Dark Sun,* says, "Knowledge derived from espionage could only speed up the process [of making a bomb], not determine it, and in fact every nation that has attempted to build an atomic weapon in the half-century since the discovery of nuclear fission has succeeded on the first try." That was not the general understanding of atomic secrets in the days of the Cold War. Nobody was above suspicion. Much in the same way that Beria's scientists were told their past accomplishments would not protect them if they didn't continue to produce, did the charismatic Oppenheimer, "Oppie," the gaunt, bony, blue-eyed genius who was the architect of the A-bomb, learn that in counseling against development of the H-bomb, he had committed a heresy for which he would be deprived of his security clearance. This was done in a public hearing that humiliated him and destroyed his spirit.

Testifying to deadly effect against him was his erstwhile physics colleague and friend, the brooding Edward Teller, once a strong advocate of international atomic controls but, at the time of his testimony, on the opposite course as the fervent promoter of—after himself—the H-bomb.

From the military ranks we will find ourselves looking more carefully at General Curtis LeMay, who after his tactical successes with the B-29s in Japan went on to the task of building the Strategic Air Command and its fleet of B-52s, some of them always in the air, bombs aboard, to "kill a nation" if the need arose. He was a patriot. He was also a blunt, tough, sometimes reckless adviser. He was, above all, a von Clausewitz of the nuclear age. He realized that with atomic weapons there is no more time inside a war. As the bomb implodes, so does time. The years-long wars of the past are compressed to moments. Thus the mobilization for war must now and forever come before the war. It follows that this blood-besotted century, having with its technology erased the distinction between combatants and noncombatants, will continue, as in the Cold War, to erase the distinction between wartime and peacetime.

On Elugelab Island on the northern end of Eniwetok Atoll in the Marshall Islands, on November 1, 1952, the hydrogen Super-bomb, code name Mike, was fired half a second before 7:15 A.M. The blast vaporized the island entirely and turned every animal, bird, and plant on the surrounding islands to cinder. The purplish fireball rose to 57,000 feet and eventually formed a canopy a hundred miles wide. "Its blast would have obliterated all New York City's five boroughs," reports Richard Rhodes. In "nanoseconds" it generated all the known elements of the universe and then created a new one. It was a thousand times more powerful than the Hiroshima bomb. It had a neutron density 10 million times greater than a supernova—"more impressive in that respect," a scientist observer said, "than a star."

The critical difference between an atom bomb and a thermonuclear bomb is that atomic fission inevitably exhausts its own chain reaction, which puts a limit on the amount of destructive power that can be built into an atom bomb. A thermonuclear bomb fired with the element of deuterium is theoretically capable of being designed to go on to the nth power. The H-bomb has no known limits.

This means we are locked up and turning in space with our Trumans and our Oppenheimers and our Fuchses and our Kurchatovs. We have closure. Until this story is written there can be no other. There is only one demand: that we select for our mythic archetypes just those scientists and politicians and generals and spies whose inadequacies of character put us most in awe of their immortal achievement.

It sits there now, conceptually finalized, a Superbomb of limitless capacity. A runaway. It does not require a plane or a submarine or an intercontinental missile to deliver it. Whoever the enemy is, wherever he is, we need only set it off where we are. Behind a barn somewhere. In the backyard.

Publication History

"Genesis" was written for the Pocket Canons Bible Series, published by Grove Press in 1999. • "E. A. Poe" is adapted from a talk given to the Poe Studies Association on October 5, 2002; passages were incorporated from the essay "Literature As Religion" in *Reporting the Universe,* published by Harvard University Press. It appeared as "Our Edgar" in the Fall 2006 issue of *VQR.* • "Harriet Beecher Stowe's Uncle Tom" is a somewhat expanded version of a review of a Stowe biography by Joan D. Hedrick, published in *The New York Times Book Review,* February 13, 1994. • "Composing *Moby-Dick:* What Might Have Happened" is an edited text of the Astman Distinguished Lecture, given before the Melville Society to celebrate the 150th anniversary of *Moby-Dick*'s publication. The lecture was published in *Leviathan: A Journal of Melville Studies,* volume 5, number 1, and reprinted in the Summer 2004 number of *The Kenyon Review.* • "Sam Clemens's Two Boys" derives from an introduction to the Oxford Mark Twain edition of *The Adventures of Tom Sawyer,* published in 1996, and from a piece on *Huckleberry Finn* published in the June 26 / July 3, 1995, issue of *The New Yorker.* • "Sinclair Lewis's *Arrowsmith*" was written as an afterword for the Signet Classic edition published in 1998. • "Fitzgerald's *Crack-Up*" was written as an introduction to a selection of Fitzgerald's autobiographical pieces published as *The Jazz Age* by New Directions in 1996. • "Malraux, Hemingway, and the Spanish Civil War" was given, in a somewhat different form, as a talk to the annual conference of the Abraham Lincoln Brigade Archives at New York University in October 2002. Parts of it derive from an earlier piece on Hemingway given originally as the Hopwood Lecture at the University of Michigan in 1985 under the title "The Beliefs of Writers." • "Dos Passos: *U.S.A.*" served as introduction to the Houghton Mifflin editions of John Dos Passos's *U.S.A.* trilogy, published in May 2000. • "Harpo" was commissioned by The Little Bookroom for their volume *Harpo Speaks . . . About New York,* a childhood reminiscence published in 2001. • "Heinrich von Kleist" was written for *The Plays of Heinrich von Kleist,* published by Continuum International. • "Arthur Miller" was published in the program of the Public Theater in New York on the occasion of the premiere of Miller's *The Ride Down Mt. Morgan,* December 1998. • "Franz Kafka's *Amerika*" was written as an introduction to the 1996 Schocken Books translation by Willa and Edwin Muir. • "W. G. Sebald" was delivered at a symposium in memory of Sebald held at Queens College, February 26, 2003. It was published in the *Los Angeles Times Book Review* of March 23, 2003. • "Einstein: Seeing the Unseen" is based on a lecture given at the Aspen Institute in the summer of 2004 for a conference celebrating the one hundredth anniversary of Einstein's birth. It was published in the December 2004 number of *Discover.* • "The Bomb" was written as a review of a number of books on nuclear weapons for the August 21, 1995, issue of *The Nation.*

About the Author

E. L. DOCTOROW's work has been published in thirty languages. His novels include *The March, City of God, Welcome to Hard Times, The Book of Daniel, Ragtime, Loon Lake, Lives of the Poets, World's Fair, Billy Bathgate,* and *The Waterworks.* Among his honors are a National Book Award, two Pen/Faulkner Awards, three National Book Critics Circle awards, the Edith Wharton Citation for fiction, the William Dean Howells Medal of the American Academy of Arts and Letters, and the presidentially conferred National Humanities Medal. He lives in New York.

BE BRAVE,
BABY RABBIT

CREATED BY LUCY BATE

STORY BY FRAN MANUSHKIN
PICTURES BY DIANE DE GROAT

Crown Publishers, Inc., New York

Text copyright © 1990 by Crown Publishers, Inc.
Illustrations copyright © 1990 Diane de Groat
All rights reserved. No part of this book may be reproduced or
transmitted in any form or by any means, electronic or
mechanical, including photocopying, recording, or by any
information storage and retrieval system, without permission in
writing from the publisher.
Published by Crown Publishers, Inc., a Random House company,
225 Park Avenue South, New York, New York 10003
CROWN is a trademark of Crown Publishers, Inc.
Manufactured in Hong Kong

Library of Congress Cataloging-in-Publication Data
Manushkin, Fran. Be brave, baby rabbit / created by Lucy Bate ;
written by Fran Manushkin ; illustrated by Diane de Groat.
p.   cm.
Summary: While playing follow-the-leader with his big sister,
Baby Rabbit can't manage to jump over a bushel basket; but, after
he stands up to a Halloween monster, he has the confidence
to make the leap.
ISBN 0-517-57573-6 (trade)—ISBN 0-517-57574-4 (lib. bdg.)
[1. Brothers and sisters—Fiction. 2. Rabbits—Fiction.] I. Bate, Lucy.
II. De Groat, Diane, ill. III. Title. PZ7.M3195Bae 1990
[E]—dc20   89-49460
CIP
AC

10 9 8 7 6 5 4 3 2 1   First Edition

For Daniel Jacobson
F.M.

One sunny Halloween the Rabbit family was out in the garden. Father and Mother Rabbit were picking apples. Little Rabbit and Baby Rabbit were playing follow the leader.

Little Rabbit walked across a log.

So did Baby Rabbit.

Little Rabbit tossed an acorn up and caught it.

And so did Baby Rabbit.

Little Rabbit said, "I bet you can't do
this!" She took a deep breath and a great
big jump—over a basket of apples.

"Sure, I can do that!" bragged Baby Rabbit. He took a deep breath and a great big jump—and tumbled to the ground. "Ouch, ouch!" he yelled, and he started to cry.

Quickly, Mother picked up Baby Rabbit and hugged him close to her. "Thank goodness it's just a scratch," said Mother. "Come inside and I'll make it better."

Very gently Mother washed the dirt off Baby Rabbit's nose and dabbed on medicine.

"I want a big bandage!" sniffled Baby Rabbit.

"Of course!" agreed Mother, and she put it on and gave him a little kiss.

Little Rabbit watched Mother kissing Baby Rabbit. "Oh, Mommy," Little Rabbit said. "Come and help me put on my costume. It's time to go trick-or-treating."

"I'm going too!" said Baby Rabbit.

"Do we have to take him?" asked Little Rabbit. "Isn't he too small?"

"I'm not too small," said Baby Rabbit.

"Of course you aren't," said Mother Rabbit. "We are all going together."

Baby Rabbit got into his lion costume. "Grrr!" he growled.

"Whoo-hoo-hoo!" Little Rabbit hooted. "I'm a brave Indian princess!"

As they all hurried out the door, Father came in carrying the basket of apples. "Have fun, everyone! By the time you are back, there'll be hot apple pie to eat."

Little Rabbit led the way to the first house. "I love Halloween! It's so spooky!" she said. Little Rabbit knocked on the door as hard as she could and shouted, "Trick or treat!"

"Mommy!" Baby Rabbit said when the door opened. "Mommy, it's a witch!"

"It's Mary Woodchuck," Mother Rabbit said, smiling. "She's wearing a costume, just like you."

"Oh!" Baby Rabbit peeked from behind his tail and put out his paw for a treat.

Then they walked to the house across the road. "Trick or treat!" called out Little Rabbit.

"Trick or treat!" echoed Baby Rabbit.

"Well, what have we here?" wondered Mrs. Squirrel. "I've never seen a lion with a bandage on."

"Baby Rabbit fell down!" Little Rabbit explained. "He fell right on his nose!"

"Ouch!" said Mrs. Squirrel. "I'll bet that hurt." She gave Baby Rabbit a pat on the head and a little bag of popcorn.

At the next house Baby Rabbit said, "I want to knock on the door this time!" And he did. He knocked as hard as he could and shouted, "Trick or treat!"

"Oh, my," said Mr. Raccoon, "what a fierce young lion." Baby Rabbit smiled proudly as Mr. Raccoon gave him a cookie. "Tell me," Mr. Raccoon said. "What happened to your nose?"

"I'll tell you what happened," said Little Rabbit.

"No!" said Baby Rabbit. "It's my nose! Don't tell!"

"You don't have to tell me," said Mr. Raccoon. "Let me see if I can guess. Were you riding on a bucking bronco, and he tossed you off his back?"

"No, no, no!" said Baby Rabbit with a little smile.

"Let me guess again," said Mr. Raccoon. "Were you rescuing Little Rabbit from a sneaky crocodile?"

"I would if I saw one!" Baby Rabbit shouted. And he leaped away with a growl.

Baby Rabbit growled all the way down the path. Suddenly he and Little Rabbit saw a huge purple monster running toward them, roaring!

"*Yeeeeek!*" Little Rabbit yelped, and hid behind a tree.

But Baby Rabbit didn't run. He glared at the monster and roared right back!

The scary monster stopped his roaring. He smiled and gave Baby Rabbit a hug. It was Grandpa Rabbit!

Baby Rabbit hugged his grandpa right back.

"My," said Little Rabbit, "You are really brave!"

"I am!" said Baby Rabbit. "I really am!"

Baby Rabbit couldn't wait to get home and tell Father Rabbit what had happened. "Daddy!" he shouted. "Trick-or-treating was scary, and it was lots of fun!"

Father nodded. "Lots of things are scary and fun!"

"I scared a monster," said Baby Rabbit proudly. "I roared and jumped all around!"

"Good for you!" Father smiled.

"Daddy, do you know what?" said Baby Rabbit. "Maybe I can jump over those apples, too!"

"I bet you can!" agreed Father.

Little Rabbit said, "On your mark, get set, go!" Baby Rabbit took a big deep breath—and jumped right over those apples!

"Hurray! You did it!" Mother and Father cheered.
"I did it!" shouted Baby Rabbit.

"Now," said Father, "how about some pie?"

"Grrr!" roared Baby Rabbit. "I'm as hungry as a lion. I'd like the biggest slice!"

And that's just what he ate.